FIRST MAP

HOW JAMES COOK CHARTED AOTEAROA NEW ZEALAND

TESSA DUDER
ILLUSTRATED BY
David Elliot

HarperCollinsPublishers

Overleaf: An impression of the brass azimuth compass made by royal instrument maker George Adams, to a design of Gowin Knight, is believed to have been used by James Cook on at least one of his Pacific voyages. Passed to Sir Joseph Banks and then a number of private owners, it was acquired in 1885 by Sir Saul Samuel, Agent General of New South Wales, and is now held in the Mitchell Library, State Library of New South Wales.

HarperCollins*Publishers*

First published in 2019
by HarperCollins*Publishers* [New Zealand] Limited
Unit D1, 63 Apollo Drive, Rosedale, Auckland 0632, New Zealand
harpercollins.co.nz

Text copyright © Tessa Duder 2019
Illustrations copyright © David Elliot 2019

Tessa Duder asserts the moral right to be identified as the author of this work and David Elliot asserts the moral right to be identified as the illustrator of this work. This work is copyright. All rights reserved. No part of this publication may be reproduced, copied, scanned, stored in a retrieval system, recorded, or transmitted, in any form or by any means, without the prior written permission of the publisher.

HarperCollins*Publishers*
Unit D1, 63 Apollo Drive, Rosedale, Auckland 0632, New Zealand
Level 13, 201 Elizabeth Street, Sydney NSW 2000, Australia
A 53, Sector 57, Noida, UP, India
1 London Bridge Street, London, SE1 9GF, United Kingdom
Bay Adelaide Centre, East Tower, 22 Adelaide Street West, 41st floor, Toronto,
    Ontario M5H 4E3, Canada
195 Broadway, New York NY 10007, USA

A catalogue record for this book is available from the National Library of New Zealand

ISBN 978 1 7755 4094 6 [hbk]

Cover and internal design by Darren Holt, HarperCollins Design Studio

Cover images: Illustrations © David Elliot; A chart of the New Zeland [Zealand] or the islands ... of the south sea. / British Library, London, UK / © British Library Board. All Rights Reserved / Bridgeman Images

Layout by Jane Waterhouse
Typeset in Historical Fell Type by Jane Waterhouse

Printed and bound in China by RR Donnelley on 157gsm matt art

8 7 6 5 4 3 2 1   19 20 21 22

Contents

Foreword	5
1. London, 12 July 1771	7
2. Bound for Tahiti	19
3. Landfall at Tūranganui-a-Kiwa	27
4. To Cape Turnagain	37
5. Among Islands	51
6. Contrary Winds	63
7. At Ship Cove	71
8. Deep South	81
9. Beyond New Zealand	95
10. The Legacy	101
Bibliography	108
Acknowledgements	110
Index	111

Foreword

In the summer of 1771 the talk of London society was the return of His Majesty's Bark *Endeavour* from her three-year voyage to the Pacific Ocean under the command of Lieutenant James Cook.

He had found no evidence of *Terra Australis Incognita*, that Great Southern Continent confidently supposed by some geographers to exist in the unexplored vastness of the Pacific. However, he had apparently shown to the Admiralty, the Royal Society and even King George, his charts of two sizeable islands in the south-west Pacific, previously unknown to European mapmakers. Abel Tasman's 1642 chart of a coastline that came to be called 'New Zeland' was now seen as just a fragment of something much more substantial, claimed by James Cook for Great Britain and firmly added to the world's maps.

This book is principally a narrative of Cook's creation of the first New Zealand chart 'in spite of all tempests' [his biographer J.C. Beaglehole's tribute]. Gales and calms were not the only challenges: to chart headlands, beaches, depths, reefs and offshore islands required navigation using [to us] primitive instruments and methods in a small and cumbersome vessel of very limited manoeuvrability. Add to these, the presence of the indigenous Māori found to live around these coasts, and the daily management of a ship and complement of ninety-one men on a voyage which must, in unfamiliar and hazardous waters, have seemed never-ending.

In the mid-twentieth century, around the bicentennial of *Endeavour*'s circumnavigation, reproductions of Cook's New Zealand chart were seen in many a New Zealand home, office or holiday cottage. This particular image appeared on postage stamps and in many publications and from them two beliefs passed into popular folklore: that James Cook created a chart acclaimed among mapmakers for its astonishing accuracy — but he made two major mistakes. The first was drawing Banks Peninsula as an island. The second was drawing Stewart Island as a peninsula, joined to the mainland of the southern island.

This second 'mistake' needs correcting. The particular chart used for the popular prints was not Cook's original, known in the British Library as Folio 16, where the north-east coast of Stewart Island and the mainland facing south are left conspicuously blank. These gaps reflect Cook's uncertainty, given what he could see from the ship and measure with any accuracy. Granted, his journal indicates that he supposed the visible high land he sailed three-quarters of the way around to be an island, but he was not sure enough to draw completed coastlines onto the chart. The strange dotted lines connecting the island to the mainland on other charts from 1771, copied from Cook, were added in later, by well-meaning engravers.

For this book we have used Folio 16 to follow *Endeavour* on her epic voyage around New Zealand. For the illustrations David Elliot has evoked the iconic images very familiar from countless books about James Cook: the Nathaniel Dance portrait, Tupaia's artwork, Sydney Parkinson's sketches of Māori warriors, their waka and carvings. The original images inspiring the artwork have been acknowledged in the captions.

Until very recently ships were referred to as 'she'. It's thought this custom derived from ships often being named after significant women in boat owners' lives, or after goddesses of mythology. Figureheads on sailing ships were often female. Perhaps there's also a notion of mariners, so much away at sea, being 'married' to their ships. Today, in the media and official documents, a ship is usually an 'it.' For this book, we felt the use of 'she' was more in keeping with James Cook's eighteenth-century world.

Also, in Cook's day, all distances were given in nautical miles. [Kilometres were first adopted by France, in 1791.] We have retained miles and when appropriate, given both. A fathom, used by eighteenth century mariners to indicate depth of water, is six feet, or just under two metres. A league is three nautical miles.

Most of the quotes used are taken directly from Cook's journal of the first voyage, 1768-1771, or from the lively journal also kept on that voyage by the naturalist Joseph Banks.

Tessa Duder
Auckland, 2019

1

London, 12 July 1771

On a warm July day, a tall solidly built man can be seen striding across the cobblestones towards The Admiralty, the imposing London headquarters of His Majesty's Royal Navy.

After so many months at sea, he's aware his general appearance is scruffy. The uniform frock coat, dragged from the back of a closet in his tiny cabin, is hot and uncomfortable. His shirt and underclothes smell of salt. His dress shoes are tight. The wig, little worn for many moons, is scratchy.

He feels all of his forty-two years. Since *Endeavour* dropped anchor in the Downs off the Kentish coast earlier in the day, he's been sitting for seven hours in a rattling horse-drawn carriage, counting off the seventy-five miles to London. Between naps, he drinks in the bright green of the countryside, a welcome change from weeks of the heaving grey Atlantic.

His leather satchel contains his journal and a number of hand-drawn charts. He believes these will provide no fresh surprises for their Lordships. Had not he sent copies many months before, on a Dutch ship departing from the hellhole of Batavia? Again from Cape Town? And yet again, *Endeavour*'s log sent from his last port-of-call, the remote island of St Helena?

He carries a letter of his own, hoping that the charts will convey to their Lordships 'a tolerable knowledge' of the places the ship has visited, and that 'the discoveries we have made, tho' not great, will Apologize for the length of the Voyage'.

But reliable word of *Endeavour*'s safe return has not yet reached their Lordships at the Admiralty. They had sent him off nearly three years earlier on a great voyage of exploration and heard nothing since but rumours. They feared sinking by the Spanish, or shipwreck. There'd been no packages arriving from Batavia or St Helena.

Ushered into the ornately decorated room, Lieutenant James Cook is warmly welcomed, with many expressions of relief. Yes, he is well, indeed glad to be home. He quickly realises that his good friend Mr Philip Stephens, Secretary to the Admiralty, is desperate for news.

Had he discovered *Terra Australis Incognita*, the populated, rich and fertile Great Southern Continent that so many learned scholars believed must exist, to counterbalance the vast landmass of Asia and Europe?

Did he carry out his orders to anchor off Matavai Bay in Tahiti and there to observe the transit of the planet Venus? And what of any further discoveries in the Pacific?

Cook is a man of unusual modesty. He knows in his heart that his true 'discoveries' amount to only a few previously uncharted islands in the vast Pacific Ocean.

Had not Samuel Wallis in the *Dolphin* come across the islands of Tahiti four years before? And over a hundred years earlier, had not Abel Tasman and his navigator François Visscher sailed up the western coastline of an unknown country they called Staete Landt [thinking it was part of South America], which Dutch mapmakers now called 'Zeelandia Nova'?

Granted, on his own recent voyage he himself had made the first chart of the long eastern coastline of New Holland [Australia], nearly losing his ship on a coral reef in the process. And he had proved that there was open sea between Australia and New Guinea. That was something.

But as for the Great Southern Continent, there remained much of the southern Pacific into which he had not taken *Endeavour*. English ships before him had searched in vain. The French were known to be in the hunt. *Terra Australis Incognita* could still exist, and ardent supporters like the prominent Scottish geographer Alexander Dalrymple proved right.

He rolls out his charts over a table. There's his own complete outline of 'New Zeland', plus sixteen others of specific stretches of coast, bays and harbours. During the circumnavigation, his young officers had assisted drawing up the charts, notably Richard Pickersgill, the master's mate and already at twenty-two a skilled cartographer and 19-year-old Isaac Smith, a cousin of Cook's wife Elizabeth, later to command his own ships and retire as a rear admiral. These charts would explain the achievements of the voyage better than any words.

There is no written reference to this scene, and it's possible that the despatch of copies of Cook's charts and journals, sent ahead from St Helena, had preceded Cook's arrival. But there's a good chance that on that July day, Philip Stephens and maybe one or two other senior naval officials were, after three years of waiting, the very first to know what James Cook and *Endeavour* had achieved.

Before them is the whole Pacific Ocean, still a vast watery expanse dotted with a few islands. There is no great landmass now drawn between Cape Horn and Tahiti. There is no land south of Tahiti, just empty ocean down to 40 degrees latitude, until … *James, what are these?*

Cook smooths out the smaller chart headed up 'New Zeland'. He allows his superiors time to digest what they are seeing: two quite large islands, their intricate coastlines almost complete. [To see this map, turn to page 100.] Do not be deceived as to their substance, he warns them — these are significant territories, similar in size to the Italian peninsula or to Great Britain herself. High mountain ranges are shown running down the northern island, called 'Aeheinomouwe', and continue down the length of the southern island, named 'Tovypoenammu'. They recognise the section of western coastline drawn by Abel Tasman, from Hokitika to Cape Maria van Diemen.

LONDON, 12 JULY 1771

This image of Cook in its many variations in engravings, stamps and bank notes has become the most iconic. James Cook, shown here in a captain's full-dress uniform, sat for three portrait painters after his second voyage. William Hodges' long-lost painting, rediscovered in 1986, is generally thought the nearest likeness. Cook's wife Elizabeth is known to have been displeased with the 'severe' portrait by John Webber, now in New Zealand's Te Papa Tongarewa Museum. [After Nathaniel Dance, 'Captain James Cook', 1776]

Looking closer, they note the names he has given to coastal features. Undoubtedly there are tributes or stories behind each one: Young Nick's Head, Poverty Bay, Hicks Bay, Cape Runaway, Hawkes Bay, Cape Kidnappers, Cape Turnagain, Bay of Plenty, Portland Island, White Island, The Mayor, Mount Edgecumbe, Mercury Bay and Isles, Cape Colville, River Thames, the Barrier Isles, Point Rodney, Hen and Chickens islands, Poor Knights Islands, Bream Head, Cape Brett, the Bay of Islands, Cavalle Isles, Mount Camel, North Cape, Gannet Isle, Sugar-Loaf Isles, Mount Egmont, Cape Palliser, Castle Point.

In the southern island, there are Admiralty Bay, Cape Jackson, Queen Charlotte's Sound, Cape Campbell, Cloudy Bay and Cape Saunders, The Traps. Two islands are named after the scientists on board, Joseph Banks and Dr Daniel Solander. Up the long and exposed western side, there's the Duskey Bay, Doubtfull Harbour, Cape Foulwind and Cape Farewell.

Philip Stephens notes with quiet pleasure, at the top of Tovypoenammu is his own name. It's there twice, given to a small island and a nearby cape.

Only at Mr Banks' insistence, Cook murmurs, did he finally agree to write on the chart, for that wide stretch of open water between the two islands, 'Cook's Straights'.

His duty done, Cook bids goodbye. The accolades had been gratifying, and he knew the news of his explorations would spread like wildfire through London's coffee houses and among the scholars and mapmakers of Europe.

But now it was time to be reunited with his wife Elizabeth and their children at Mile End, five miles' walk away in east London. Sorrow awaited him as well as joy: the youngest, Elizabeth, born 1776, had died three months before his return, aged only four. And another baby, Joseph, born the day Cook sailed from Plymouth three years earlier, had lived only eighteen days.

For the moment, all thoughts of *Endeavour* and whatever he'd achieved during his long absence from his family were gone.

What great quest prompts a 39-year-old family man to leave his pregnant wife and three young children and set off in a small ship for a hazardous voyage around the world?

Why was James Cook chosen to lead this expedition, ahead of older captains of greater experience and reputation?

And how could he so accurately fix the position and coastlines of two large islands so isolated in a vast ocean?

With the new, improved sextants, navigators out of sight of land could now determine their latitude — the distance north or south from the Equator — with great accuracy. However, there was not yet any simple or reliable way to determine longitude — the distance east or west. This required an extremely accurate timekeeper, and it would not be until Cook's second voyage in 1772 that a chronometer accurate, small and robust enough to take on board a ship would be available.

Let's go back a few years, to August 1768, when a London newspaper announced that a Lieutenant James Cook and his ship *Endeavour* were waiting at Plymouth for fair winds to leave on a long voyage to the Pacific Ocean.

Its purpose had been given out by the Navy and Cook himself as merely proceeding to Tahiti. There he would observe the passing of the planet Venus across the face of the sun. Cook's observations would be one of several taken around the world, with the results used by scientists to measure the precise distance of planet Earth from the sun. Opportunities were extremely rare — the next transit was calculated to be more than a hundred years away.

Very likely, mused the reporter, there was a *second* reason for *Endeavour*'s voyage: to discover the Great Southern Continent in the Pacific, lying south of the equator from about 60 degrees latitude. The Dutch explorer Abel Tasman and his navigator François Jacobszoon Visscher in 1642 had drawn perhaps a modest fraction of its western or northern coast. Cook's secret orders could be to find the rest and take possession for His Majesty King George III. [We might add, knowing our history, for the further benefit of commerce and trade, and the growing political power of the British Empire.]

This was a time of intense scientific curiosity. Britain and her wealthy European rivals sent out explorers to find new lands, new species of plants and trees, perhaps even gold. Doctors were beginning to understand that fresh foods and especially citrus fruit could prevent scurvy, the cause of so many sailors' protracted and agonising deaths at sea.

There was also still much to discover in astronomy and geography. So, early in 1768, the learned men of the Royal Society, supported by King George and the Royal Navy, decided to send a ship to the islands of Tahiti, the ideal position in the southern hemisphere to observe the transit of Venus. The famed geographer Alexander Dalrymple, obsessed with his belief that a Great Southern Continent was waiting to be discovered, announced he would command the expedition. No, said the Navy, he most certainly would not! This idea was 'totally repugnant'. Any ship of His Majesty's Navy would be commanded only by a qualified captain of many years' experience.

They already knew the ideal person, a mariner unknown outside the inner circles of the Admiralty but respected as a fine seaman unusually competent in the sciences of astronomy, mathematics and especially in surveying and the making of charts. Granted, farmer's son James Cook lacked the support of wealthy patrons, who often ensured that less able lieutenants were promoted to captain's rank before their more competent peers. But his achievements in Canada and Newfoundland had brought him to the attention of influential men like Philip Stephens and Hugh Palliser, soon to become Comptroller of the Navy. There were undoubtedly others, older, more experienced and better-connected captains being considered, but in the end, Cook was simply the best candidate for the job.

James Cook had gained his reputation in the Navy by most unusual means. He had not come from a well-to-do family, serving in his teens as midshipman, then junior lieutenant, with good connections and the hope of rising one day to captain. He had not even learned his basic seamanship in the Royal Navy.

Born in 1728, he grew up on a farm in Yorkshire, and attended village schools, showing an unusual proficiency for mathematics. At seventeen he was apprenticed to a grocer's shop in the fishing port of Staithes. Eighteen months later, he decided he'd rather be a sailor than a shopkeeper and began as crew on the sturdy coal-carrying ships of Captain James Walker, a respected ship owner based at Whitby on the North Yorkshire coast.

By 1755, aged twenty-seven, he was experienced enough in seamanship, navigation and mathematics for Captain Walker to offer James Cook his first command. Shrewdly, he decided instead that to an ambitious mariner the Royal Navy offered many more opportunities: chances of promotion, action in battle, voyages of exploration and the possibility of handsome prize money for captains and officers. This meant enlisting at the lowly rank of able seaman, but within a few weeks he was promoted to master's mate. Only two years later came a further promotion to master, the warrant officer responsible to the captain for navigation and the ship's overall management.

On the H.M.S. *Pembroke* he crossed the Atlantic, and spent most of the next ten years in Canadian waters. He saw action against the French, and began to use his navigational expertise for the special skill of surveying, making astonishingly accurate charts of the St Lawrence River and the coastlines of Newfoundland and Halifax Harbour in Nova Scotia.

By 1768, his reputation as a fine seaman, navigator, and especially a brilliant surveyor, was sufficient for their Lordships to offer him command of H.M.B. *Endeavour*.

It was a daring appointment. Cook's only previous command was of the much smaller schooner *Grenville*, carrying just eighteen crew. His oceangoing experience was limited to the seas around Britain, the Baltic and across the Atlantic. This was considerably less than two of his officers, the American John Gore [who'd been twice around the world already] and Lieutenant Zachary Hickes, along with the master, Robert Molyneux and the master's mate, Charles Clerke. But everyone had much more to learn about the unknown eastern shores of New Holland and Tasman's sketchy fragment of Zeelandia Nova.

If there really was a great southern continent, Cook would be the man to explore and chart its coasts.

The Bark *Endeavour* was also an unlikely choice, a three-year-old Whitby collier of white oak and elm, 368 tons, 97 feet, one inch [29.6 metres] long, 29 feet [8.8 metres] wide. She was designed to carry large loads of coal and when fully laden, her draught [depth in the water] was about 14 feet [4.3 metres]. Her original name was the *Earl of Pembroke*, and she was ship-rigged, meaning square yards and sails on all three masts.

The Navy favoured a collier over a faster and more glamorous naval ship, say a frigate like Samuel Wallis's *Dolphin*. Happily, Cook had spent his formative years in Whitby colliers. He knew a collier's comparatively shallow draught would make her the safer vessel in unfamiliar coastal waters. Her flat bottom meant she could be beached for repairs and cleaning. If she ran aground she was more likely to float off. [Later in the voyage, the decision proved sound, when *Endeavour* narrowly escaped disaster on Australia's Great Barrier Reef.] Although slow, not easily manoeuvrable, she was sturdy and spacious below decks for stowage of gear and supplies. The crew fared less well, sleeping and eating in cramped and ill-lit conditions with low headroom.

Even more unusual on this naval voyage was the addition of Joseph Banks and his party. Banks was a stupendously wealthy young aristocrat and amateur botanist who determined that *his* Grand Tour would not be just around Europe ['every blockhead does that'] but be on *Endeavour* 'around the whole globe!' He shared Alexander Dalrymple's conviction that a Great Southern Continent must exist. Having promised some ten thousand pounds to secure a berth on the expedition, he advised the Royal Society, the Navy and Cook that he would also bring a fellow botanist, Dr Daniel Solander, and a secretary, Herman Spöring. Also, he had hired two artists [Sydney Parkinson for botanical specimens, Alexander Buchan for drawing landscapes], plus two footmen and two black servants from his estates. And there'd be two dogs, one his cherished greyhound.

Now the expedition had three scientific purposes: advancements in geography, astronomy and natural history.

As preparations continued, all Cook's management skills were needed. Whitby colliers usually carried only about twenty crew; *Endeavour* would depart with eighty-five crew, with Banks and his contingent, ninety-four in all.

Some sailors were taken on for their skill as carpenters, sailmakers, riggers, armourers, coopers, barbers, cooks and bakers. Twelve were marines, musket-carrying naval infantry, needed for tense situations either aboard or on shore.

Most on board were in their twenties. The youngest were the surgeon's personal servant, eleven-year-old Nicholas Young, and the master's servant, Isaac Manley, a year older. The oldest was probably the sailmaker John Ravenhill, ten years older than Cook, and a man who liked his drink.

ENDEAVOUR GENERAL:

Name:	*Endeavour*
Operator:	Royal Navy
Builder:	Thomas Fishburn, Whitby
Cost:	c. £11,800 [including refits before sale]
Launched:	June 1764
Acquired by Navy:	28 March 1768 as *Earl of Pembroke*
Commissioned:	26 May 1768
Decommissioned:	September 1774
Out of service:	March 1775, sold for £645
Renamed:	*Lord Sandwich*, February 1776
Homeport:	Plymouth, UK
Fate:	Scuttled Newport, Rhode Islands, 1778

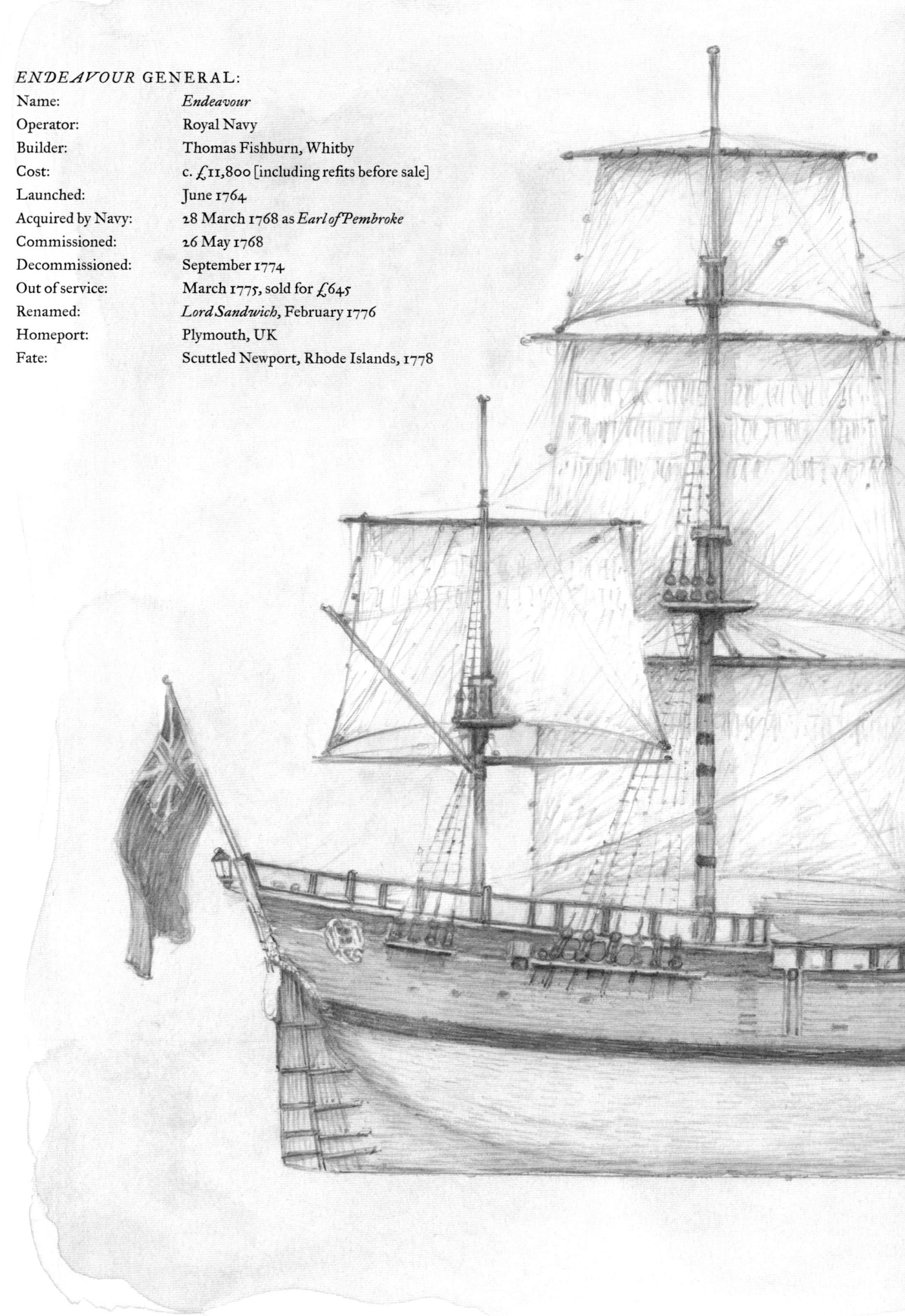

ENDEAVOUR SPECIFICATIONS:

Class and type:	Bark
Tons burthen:	368
Length waterline:	97ft 8in [29.77m]
Length extreme:	143.5ft 5in [43.7m] end bowsprit to end stern
Beam:	29ft 2in [8.89m]
Draught:	11ft 10in [3.6m]
Depth in hold:	11ft 4in [3.45m]
Height of mizzenmast:	78ft 9in [24m]
Height of mainmast:	127ft 11in [39m]
Height of foremast:	109ft 10in [33m]
Sails:	3,321 square yards [2.777m] of sail
Speed:	7—8 knots [13 to 15 km/h] maximum
Boats carried:	yawl, pinnace, longboat, two skiffs
Complement:	71 ship's company; 12 marines; 11 civilians. Total 94
Armament:	10 four-pounder cannons, 12 swivel guns

At the naval dockyard at Deptford, on the River Thames near London, carpenters toiled below decks on major alterations. The gentlemen of Banks' party required 'proper' accommodation for themselves and an extraordinary amount of scientific equipment. So did Charles Green, the astronomer hired to observe, along with Cook, the transit of Venus.

Then there was all the ship's necessary gear: spare anchors, spars, sails, great coils of rope, many wooden casks to hold water, oars and rigs for the five small boats, tools, timber, nails, paint, coal and wood for the galley fire, cannons and muskets, ammunition, spare clothing, medical supplies, plus quantities of 'trifles' as gifts for the 'natives'.

In the great cabin, an extensive library was assembled. For Cook and the officers, accounts of earlier explorers' journals, atlases and charts, and mathematical tables; for the scientists, the latest illustrated volumes of botany and zoology. Also put on board were writing materials like ink, watercolours and graphite pencils, along with a large quantity of paper: writing paper for the officers, crew and scientists keeping journals, and heavier linen-backed paper suitable for the charts that Cook and his assistants expected to produce.

Cook, as captain and [in those days] also purser, was responsible for calculating, ordering and supervising careful stowage of food supplies in the holds.

For nearly a hundred people for eighteen months, these included 34,000 pounds of bread, 9000 pounds of flour, 10,000 pieces of salted beef and pork, plus huge quantities of ship's biscuits, butter, oatmeal, wheat, sugar, oil, vinegar, malt, suet, raisins, a jellied ['portable'] soup and salted cabbage ['sour Kraut'] which Cook believed would help prevent scurvy.

Then there were the animals. Plenty of feed was needed for Banks' two dogs, a few cats and, penned up on deck, cows, chickens, ducks, pigs, sheep and a milk-goat.

The sailors would catch fish, of course, to supplement food rations, but for water Cook must rely on freshwater streams ashore to fill the many wooden casks. [While at sea they don't seem to have used spare sails or buckets to catch rainwater.] They would also need to collect wood for the galley's stove and gather edible fresh greens, as further protection from scurvy.

Besides foodstuffs, there was [to us] an astonishing amount of alcohol loaded into the holds, for both officers and men. The officers and scientists drank spirits and wine. The sailors lined up for their morning ration of grog, a mixture of rum, water and sugar, and were entitled to eight pints of beer a day. This was safer to drink than water as it kept for longer in wooden casks.

At sea, mariners were often cold, wet, hungry, short on sleep and altogether bone-weary. They needed to be tough. Cook preferred the three-watch system which allowed the sailors eight hours of continuous sleep, but in any kind of heavy weather more men were required on deck and a two-watch system allowed only four hours in their hammocks.

Working aloft was a dangerous activity, even in calm weather. In storms and navigating through unknown coastal waters, sailors handling heavy, sodden square sails high up on the yards feared for the ship and for their lives. In calms, they had to endure long days of frustration and boredom. They got on each other's nerves. Alcohol made life more bearable.

PROCEEDING SOUTH

On 8 August 1768 *Endeavour* sailed down the English Channel in a fresh north-westerly, passing the legendary white cliffs of Dover and Beachy Head before anchoring in Plymouth to embark botanists Joseph Banks and Dr Daniel Solander.

Cook's chart of Otaheite resulted from his six-day circumnavigation of Otaheite Nui and the smaller Otaheite Iti, accompanied by Joseph Banks and a Tahitian guide, Tauhu. Joining the party halfway through, Tupaia introduced them to several chiefs and showed them the impressive 12-metre stone pyramid of the great marae of Mahaiatea, on the south-western coast near Papara.
National Library of Australia

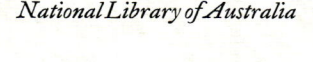

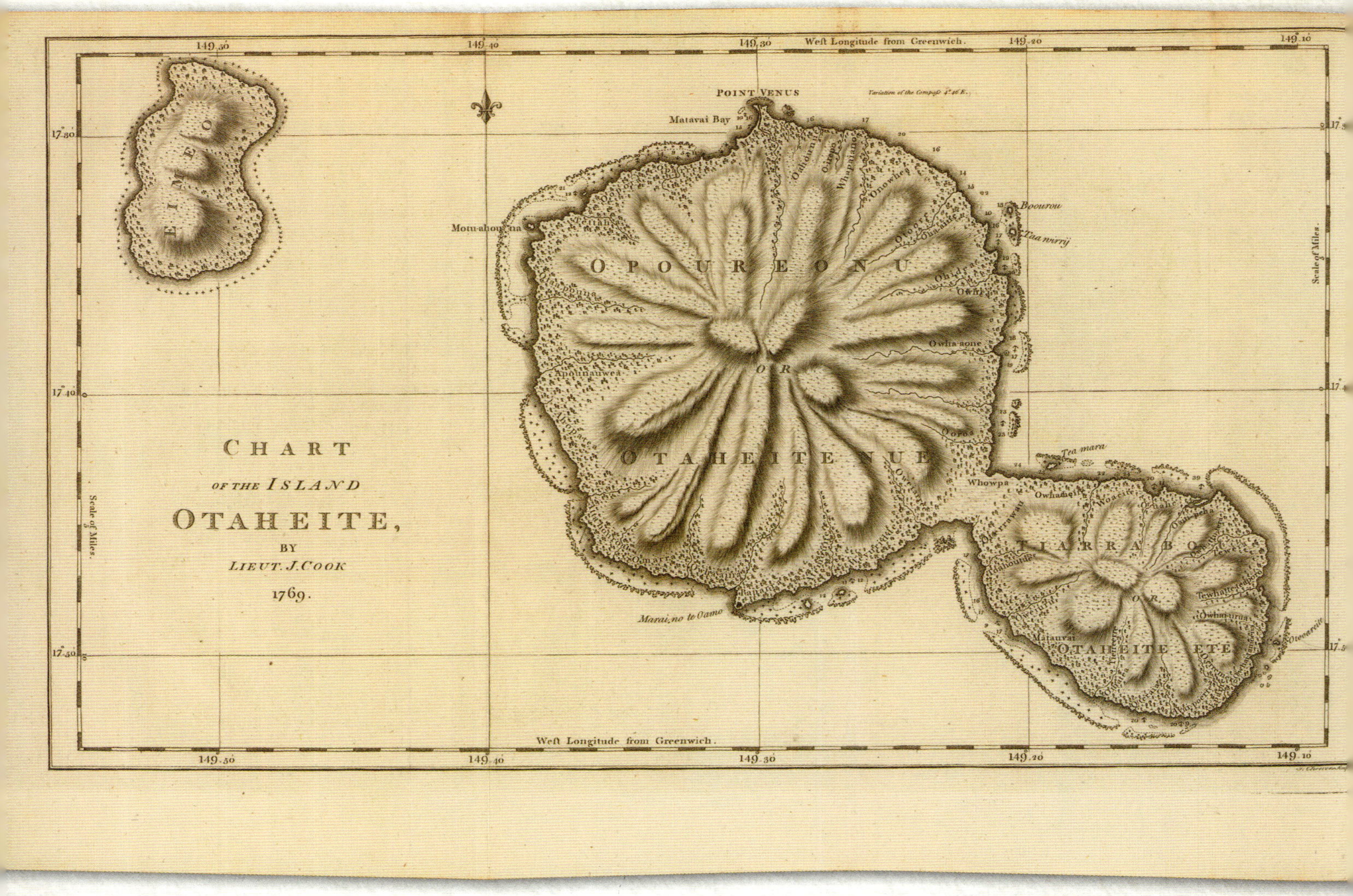

2

Bound for Tahiti

On 30 July 1768, the heavily-laden *Endeavour* headed down the Thames Estuary and into the English Channel.

At Plymouth they picked up Joseph Banks and his entourage and within two days, ship, crew and no doubt many seasick passengers were weathering their first full-blown North Atlantic gale.

In his cabin, Cook had stowed away two sets of official instructions. The first ordered him simply to proceed to Tahiti and there, on the known date of 3 June 1769, to observe the transit of Venus.

The second set of orders — *not to be opened until after Tahiti* — directed him to proceed southward until he reached a latitude of 40 degrees, unless he had already found land.

If not, he should proceed westward until he reached the eastern coast of New Holland or *Terra Australis Incognita*, so far unknown to Europeans. Failing that, he should proceed to 'the Eastern side of the Land discover'd in 1642 by Tasman and now called New Zeland'. There he should fully describe what he found and cultivate good relations with the inhabitants.

Cook also carried another set of instructions, written by the Earl of Morton, President of the Royal Society which had sponsored the expedition.

The Earl had no doubt read disturbing passages in the journals of Captain Samuel Wallis, describing his visit to Tahiti in H.M.S. *Dolphin* two years earlier, the first by a European ship. Though good relationships were later established, initial conflict with the natives of Matavai Bay had resulted in Tahitian deaths and the savage destruction, on Wallis's order, of some eighty canoes.

In his 'Hints', Morton advised Cook that any 'natives' encountered should be treated with 'the utmost patience and forbearance'. The sailors and 'wanton use' of firearms should be checked. The shedding of native blood was 'a crime of the highest nature'; they were as much human creatures of God as 'the most polished Europeans'.

Equally, they were 'the legal possessors of the several Regions they inhabit,' and no European Nation had the right to occupy or settle any part of their country 'without their voluntary consent'.

True to his times, the good earl believed that there were many ways to convince natives of 'the Superiority of Europeans'. If, during an inevitable skirmish, some natives should be slain, the survivors [the Europeans] should understand that their motive was only of self-defence. But he repeated, natives, 'when brought under, should be treated with distinguished humanity'. They should be made aware that 'the Crew still considers them as Lords of the Country'.

Though to us patronising, these were at the time considered lofty, humane ideals, in keeping with the period of European history known as the Enlightenment. The shipboard journals of both James Cook and Joseph Banks make it clear that these 'Hints' were taken to heart — even if, in the heat of the moment, they proved sometimes difficult to put into practice.

On 12 September, *Endeavour* reached the island of Madeira, and in mid-November put in to Rio de Janeiro to stock up on food, wine and water.

Ahead lay the challenge of rounding Cape Horn. Rather than pass through the Strait of Magellan, Cook chose the longer route to the Pacific, taking *Endeavour* through Le Maire Strait, between Tierra del Fuego and Isla de los Estados.

With *Endeavour* anchored for a last-chance opportunity to collect wood, fresh water and a wild and plentiful edible green [possibly a form of sow thistle] called 'sellery', Banks led an expedition of eleven men ashore, resulting in the tragic deaths of his two black servants. High up in the snow-covered hills, suffering from exposure and the effects of a bottle of rum, they could not be moved with the scientists to lower levels. Next day they were discovered to have frozen to death.

On 25 January, *Endeavour* set a course for Cape Horn. Mariners doubling the Horn west-about into the prevailing winds always expected a mighty battle, but for his first rounding, Cook was unusually fortunate. The weather gods served up plenty of strong winds, but he was still able to carry close to full sail.

Indeed, the sighting of the infamous cape out to starboard was clear enough for Cook and Charles Green to calculate its longitude very accurately. They used both the sun and the new, more complicated lunar method recently introduced by the Astronomer Royal, Nevil Maskelyne. This required about four hours of laborious mathematical calculations, a procedure that Cook had been one of the first navigators in the Navy to master.

Cook now turned *Endeavour* northwest towards Tahiti. On his passage from Cape Horn to Tahiti, Samuel Wallis in the *Dolphin* had not sighted any land. Perhaps, Joseph Banks must be thinking as he gazed at the empty horizon, the glory of discovering the fabled southern continent might still be theirs.

We know from his journals that Cook was more sceptical.

Endeavour dropped anchor in Matavai Bay on 13 April 1769. Since leaving Rio de Janiero, the voyage had been long enough for the first signs of scurvy to have appeared [unusual fatigue and sore gums], so Cook ordered sauerkraut and meat soup to be served. At first the sailors refused to eat the sour pickled cabbage, but they changed their minds when told it was on the officers' table. It must be good!

To sailors who'd seen nothing but sea for weeks, sun-drenched Matavai Bay seemed like paradise. Warm breezes, welcoming canoes, palm-shaded beaches. After stodgy ship food, exotic treats like sweet potatoes, sugar cane, coconuts, bananas and breadfruit were delicious and plentiful.

The visit began peaceably enough, with brisk trading of small items between the sailors and locals. They learned basic words and phrases of each other's language. One Tahitian word entered English: *tatau* or tattoo. The sailors, even Banks, eagerly acquired tattoos of their own, starting a trend for 'tattowing' that later spread through the whole British navy.

Inevitably, officers, sailors and scientists alike formed relationships with local women. As a married man, Cook busied himself elsewhere. He exchanged gifts with the chiefs, or went off exploring in one of the small boats. With Banks and Tauhu, a Tahitian guide, he circumnavigated Tahiti and produced a splendid chart of the island. He and Green directed preparations for the approaching astronomical observations. Precision instruments provided by the Royal Society needed to be taken ashore, set up on the flat area known as Port Venus, and tested: the larger included a theodolite [a surveyor's instrument for measuring angles], telescopes, compasses, an astronomical quadrant, thermometers and clocks.

But from the start there were signs of strain. With the sailors preferring to spend much of their time ashore, rather than attending to work on the ship, discipline and good health became harder to maintain.

Cook had drawn up some 'Rules', based on the Earl of Morton's 'Hints', to guide his men towards respectful dealings with the locals, but they hardly reckoned on the Tahitians' cheerful pilfering of items from the ship, even from sailors' pockets. Certain valuables like knives, tools and jackets, even part of one instrument needed for their coming observation of Venus — these were all vital and irreplaceable.

Exasperation and growing mutual distrust led to some tense situations. Nevertheless, on 3 June the transit of Venus was dutifully observed by Green, Cook and Solander, with hazy conditions producing disappointing results.

Despite all Cook's good intentions, relationships with the islanders worsened. With two of his men injured in a scuffle and pilfering increasing, Cook was persuaded it was time to leave Tahiti, prompting two marines to desert. They were found some way inland and forcibly returned to the ship, but only after a tense two-day stand-off with the Tahitians, which involved the taking of hostages on both sides and Cook angrily threatening severe punishment.

				Opatoero

N

Oahourou Oryvavai Olematerea Oateeu Orurutu
          Orarathoa   Oahoo-ahoo
                                          Ooureu   Motuhea
   Toutepa   Oweha
                                          Whennua ouda
                                  Opopotea
  toe miti no terara te rietea   Ma-
       Orivavie   -rua
                    Orotuma
   Tinuna   Opoopooa

Tereati
Toottera W——————————————————————————————Eavat

   Ohetepoto   Tetupatupa eahow
                                  Moenatayo
   Ohetetoutou-atu

   Ohetetoutou-mi
                         Teerrepooopomathehea Oheavie

                                                   Opooroo

   Ohetetoutoureva
                                          Teoroorouiatiwa- Oouow
                                          -tea

   Ohetetaiteare
                                                   Otootoo

       Teamoorohete   Teatowhete
                                                   Onowhe

S

Opato

Tupaia's 'Chart of the South Pacific' is often attributed to James Cook based on information provided by Tupaia, but Cook's journal notes that it was 'drawn by Tupia's own hands'. Scholars believe the islands, with Tahiti at the centre, are laid out to reflect distances and routes. The original chart has not survived but a copy is held at the British Library, London.
British Library

It was a sad ending to the visit. Cook wrote in his journal of his disappointment that the two deserters had caused *Endeavour* to be leaving the Tahitians 'in disgust with our behaviour towards them'.

Nevertheless, most of the chiefs and their families came to the beach to farewell Cook and his ship. Many canoes put out from the shore just as they had done three months earlier. Quite a few tears, British and Tahitian, were shed.

For one man and a boy, as *Endeavour* sailed from Matavai Bay, it was to prove their last sighting of the group of islands they called home.

Among the Tahitians whom Cook had come to know well was Tupaia, a high priest and renowned navigator whose noble bearing and intellectual curiosity had impressed both Cook and Banks.

Though Cook was reluctant, Banks had encouraged the idea of Tupaia travelling on with *Endeavour* to England, under his patronage. Tupaia also brought a servant, a small boy named Taiata — who probably soon made friends with Nick Young and Isaac Manley.

Scarlet hibiscus and other tropical flowers, fruits and vegetables awaited *Endeavour*'s weary sailors on arrival at Tahiti's Matavai Bay. Joseph Banks described the island's lush vegetation and spectacular mountain backdrop as 'the truest form of arcadia.' [After Sydney Parkinson, 'Hibiscus rosa-sinensis', 1769.]

And so, as *Endeavour* left Matavai Bay, Tupaia gave Cook directions for the island of Huahine and then his own birthplace, the sacred island of Ra'iātea. Some years earlier it had been invaded by people from the nearby island of Bora Bora, and Tupaia gravely wounded.

At Ra'iātea the ship and crew were greeted enthusiastically, with musical entertainments and marae visits. Cook also noted the boathouses sheltering large ocean-going canoes. These vessels, he speculated, could explain the mystery of how the vast Pacific was peopled, perhaps from as far away as the East Indies.

Imagine, then, these two men standing side-by-side on *Endeavour*'s poop deck as she reaches open sea. They are a similar age: Tupaia is about forty-five, the older by five years. They converse in a halting mixture of Tahitian and English. Both are accomplished navigators but from very different traditions.

As an experienced seafarer, Cook is always alert to seasonal changes, to clouds, wind directions, sea states, tides, currents and birdlife, but to fix his ship's position and plot courses on paper he relies on science: his state-of-the-art instruments and knowledge of astronomy and mathematics. And some help is available, at least as far as Cape Horn and Tahiti: in the great cabin he has copies of the charts and journals of previous European explorers.

Tupaia has no precision instruments, no compass or sextant or written charts. To set a course between known islands, he relies on his long experience of the ocean's natural environment: the seasonal changes, the paths of the moon, sun and stars, the characteristics and patterns of the clouds, winds and waves. He's alert to what sea birds and other marine life can tell him. He listens to the voices of his ancestors.

Tupaia is generous with his knowledge and from his journal it is clear that Cook, taking *Endeavour* among these unfamiliar islands, is glad to have him on board. Tupaia gives Banks the names of 130 known islands and for Cook draws an extraordinary Pacific chart of his own, placing Ra'iātea at the centre of more than 70 islands as far flung as Tonga and Samoa.

As *Endeavour* prepares to leave the archipelago, Tupaia naturally wants Cook to sail westwards, among the islands he himself has already visited: Tonga, probably Samoa, others still unknown to Europeans. But as a well-trained naval officer, Cook dutifully obeys orders and he has his strict Admiralty instructions: from Tahiti he will proceed directly south to the latitude of 40 degrees.

He already knows, from Tupaia and the voyages of Abel Tasman and Samuel Wallis, that to the west of the Tahiti island group lies no great landmass. If it is anywhere, it will be south.

3

Landfall at Tūranganui-a-Kiwa

Seven long weeks passed. After a brief visit to Rurutu in the Austral Islands, no land was sighted. Colder weather saw Tupaia and Taiata don European clothing and the sailors their heavy woollen fearnought jackets.

In the great cabin, Banks and his team spent the days cataloguing and sketching their already large collection of plants, birds and marine life. Normally, this sizeable cabin at the stern was a captain's private sanctuary, where he kept his charts, journals and instruments and was served meals alone, but Banks was no respecter of naval tradition. For working on his charts Cook maintained a minimal presence.

On deck, officers and crew constantly scanned the horizon, finding only 'Cape Flyaway', which always turned out to be banks of clouds or tricks of the light. They saw a comet, rainbows, and many large birds including albatrosses, shearwaters and petrels. Despite contrary winds, gales and vicious squalls, *Endeavour* ploughed on, ever further south.

At 40 degrees latitude, on 2 September and seeing 'not the least visible signs of land', Cook had had enough.

In better weather he might have continued, but his crew was tired and the 'great swells' from the south were telling him there was no landmass in that direction. So he turned the ship northwards, then southwest. Around that latitude, sooner or later, he would surely meet up with the land shown on Tasman's chart.

By the end of September excitement was mounting. To Cook, Tupaia and all on board, there were definite signs of land. A seal. Seaweed. Pieces of barnacled wood. Unfamiliar birds. A great many albatrosses and 'porpoisses'.

The sea was definitely a paler colour, meaning less depth of water, though even at 180 fathoms [1080 feet, 329 metres] the lead weight thrown frequently by the linesman was still not touching bottom.

Cook promised a gallon of rum [about 4.5 litres] to whoever first sighted land by day, or two gallons if at night — and further, the spotter's own name would be given to some part of the coast.

Were they, at last, after a voyage of fifteen months, about to sight the fabled Great Southern Continent, *Terra Australis Incognita*?

Up until this point, Cook had taken *Endeavour* into ports and harbours for which there were charts, of sorts, and accounts written by earlier explorers.

'New Zeland' is different. For probably the first time in his twenty-two years at sea, he is approaching a coast of which he knows next to nothing. Tasman had described his landfall near Hokitika as 'a large land, uplifted high', and sailing north he'd seen out to starboard more high land, though not the snow-clad peak Cook was to call Mount Egmont.

But Tasman's navigator François Visscher had charted a *western* coast of something. This, triumphantly spotted by Nick Young perched up on the masthead in the early afternoon of 7 October 1769, is an *eastern* coast — of what, precisely?

Cook and his lieutenants train their telescopes on the wide bay ahead. It's a bright spring day, and the ship is running before gentle easterlies. Cook's journal notes the steep cliffs, the green hilly countryside with high mountains inland. It's certainly inhabited: in the bay are several canoes, with people walking on the shore and behind them, houses.

What's going through his mind as *Endeavour* slowly approaches the coast? Surely intense excitement, pride, relief! But also apprehension — he urgently needs to send men ashore for much-needed wood, water and anti-scurvy greens. He knows of Tasman's hostile reception in 'Murderer's Bay', when four men sent ashore for the same reason did not make it back to the ship. Tasman had left New Zealand without setting foot on it.

Will these people be as friendly as the Tahitians? Are these people on the beach Polynesians? Some other race? *Tupaia, is that fencing of wooden spikes possibly fortifications enclosing a village?*

There are other reasons for his anxiety. As a surveyor, Cook is impatient to begin charting this wide bay, the headlands and what lies beyond to north and south. [He isn't to know that New Zealand's coastline is some 8,700 miles [14,000 kms, or by some measures up to 18,000], the tenth longest coastline of any country.]

His cumbersome ship, with its relatively inefficient square sails and small jib staysails, is at the mercy of the winds, the tides, and her captain's skill and judgement. Cook is very aware that she can make way through the water only with the wind coming from astern, or from just ahead of right angles to the hull. This significantly limits her manoeuvrability. An accurate

Nicholas Young's sighting of the mountains to the south of Tūranganui-a-Kiwa. On hearing the shout of 'Land!' all hands rushed on deck, confident that they had found the Great Southern Continent. The boy's reward was a gallon of rum and his name given to the head forming the southern arm of Tūranganui-a-Kiwa/Poverty Bay: Young Nick's Head.

Artists Sydney Parkinson and Herman Spöring drew numerous coastal profiles during *Endeavour*'s circumnavigation. This shows the Tūranganui-a-Kiwa coast, with one of the thirteen large fires shown in Spöring's larger panorama of Poverty Bay, drawn while *Endeavour* was at anchor there. Fires were customarily used by Māori to clear ground, but here may have been lit as signals to nearby hapu. [After Herman Spöring, sketch of 'Taoneroa', 1769.]

chart requires close observation of the coastal features, but equally, means a captain taking great risks. Being caught on a lee shore in a gale will likely end in shipwreck. In calmer seas, a captain can launch the small boats for his terrified sailors to tow the ship away from danger, or as a last resort, drop anchor.

For safe navigation along these unfamiliar coasts, Cook has only the three L's — lead, latitude and lookout. The *lead* is a cone-shaped weight [about 7 lbs or just over 3 kilograms] swung by a linesman into the water; how much of the 200 fathoms [365 metres] of line goes out indicates the depth beneath the hull.

Latitude is the north–south position of the ship on the Earth's surface, relative to the equator [0 degrees] and north or south poles [90 degrees]. For creating a chart, Cook must constantly take sightings with a sextant, even several times daily, to note down *Endeavour*'s position, her course and the coastline's features.

And *lookout* means the sharp eyes of his sailors posted at the masthead or bowsprit day and night, whatever the weather. It is their job to scan the seas ahead for submerged reefs, isolated rocks, unusual wave patterns or the warning sound of breaking surf — *anything* that indicates possible danger.

Today, it's not danger that the sharp eyes of Nicholas Young have spotted, earning him his gallon of rum [which he shares out], but the purple smudge of distant land: unmistakeably high mountains behind the wide bay and its headlands. Young Nick's Head is one of the first coastal features his captain writes on the blank sheet of paper to become the 'New Zeland' chart.

Two days pass before Cook cautiously brings *Endeavour* to anchor in the bay first sighted, about two kilometres from the shore. The bay itself, known to the local people as Tūranganui-a-Kiwa, is a deep horseshoe. He can see a river mouth, surely a source of good clean water.

He has not come to invade these islands, nor to colonise them, nor even to 'discover', since the 'Indians' he can see ashore have already done so, possibly many centuries earlier.

His orders are clear: explore, chart and describe the land; cultivate a friendship with the inhabitants; and gain their consent for possession to be taken of convenient situations in the country for King George III.

Though it will be several decades before whalers, British missionaries and finally British colonists arrive, on this bright October day in 1769 the future of the numerous and well-established people living round the shores of these two large islands that came to be known as Aotearoa was undeniably, and forever, altered.

However excited Cook and his men were that day, nothing could have matched the astonishment of the men, women and children on shore. One famous account speaks of people crying out that the sails of this travelling island were like clouds in the sky. Some thought it was a legendary bird, godlike.

Then they saw a smaller bird descending into the water, along with some beings apparently of human shape. For the families living with their hapu in well-established pā along the coasts

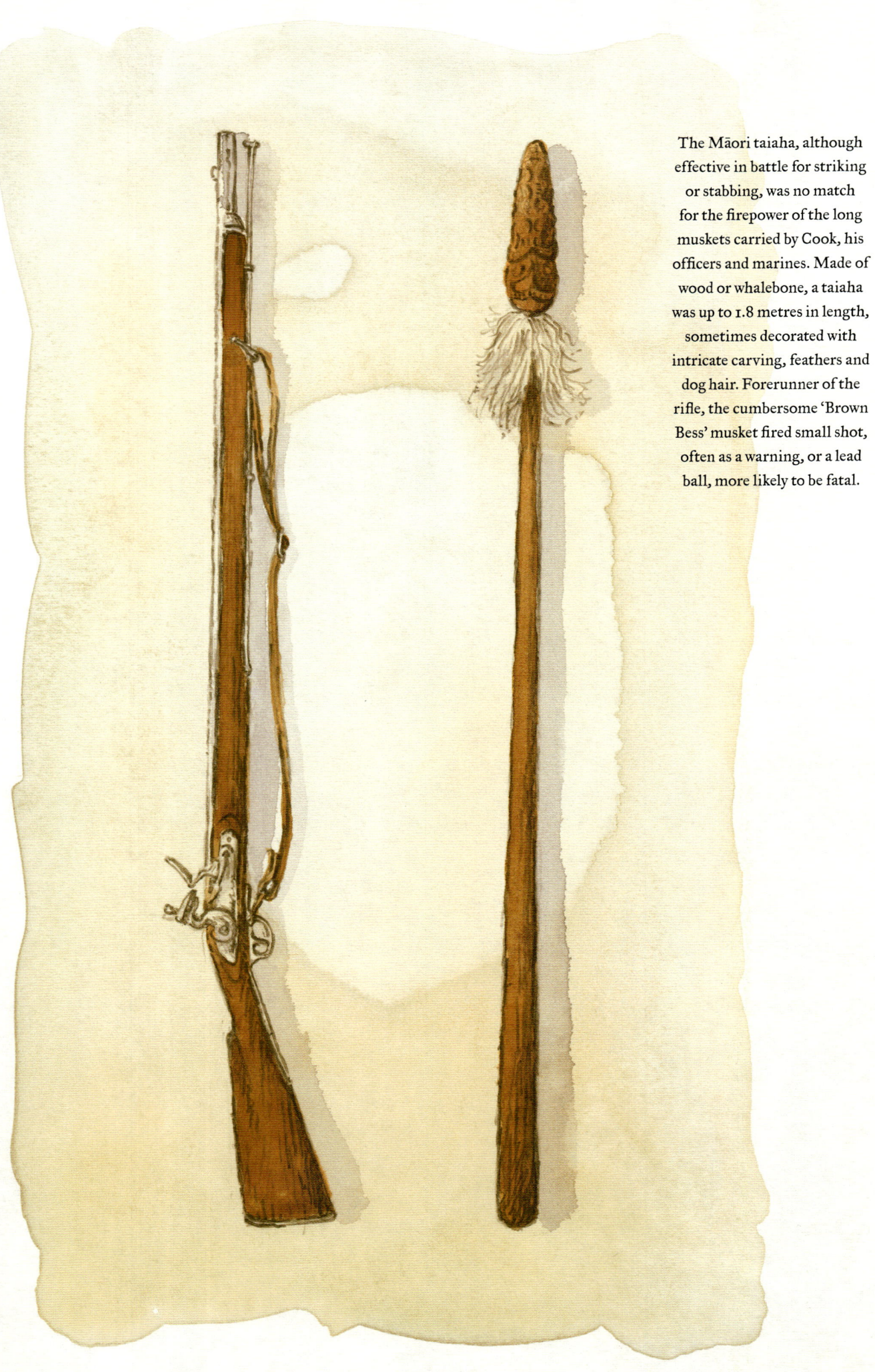

The Māori taiaha, although effective in battle for striking or stabbing, was no match for the firepower of the long muskets carried by Cook, his officers and marines. Made of wood or whalebone, a taiaha was up to 1.8 metres in length, sometimes decorated with intricate carving, feathers and dog hair. Forerunner of the rifle, the cumbersome 'Brown Bess' musket fired small shot, often as a warning, or a lead ball, more likely to be fatal.

of Aotearoa, *Endeavour*'s arrival would have been akin to a visitation from space, utterly beyond imagining.

And what of Tupaia, as he stands on *Endeavour*'s deck, watching two boats go ashore carrying Cook, Lieutenant Gore, Banks and his scientists, four boys and a party of red-coated marines.

Is he wondering how alike these people are to himself? Are their weapons, their clothing, their homes, canoes and marae in any way similar? Their language — maybe he can understand it? Is that smoke on the hills coming from signal fires to alert the people to intruders? *Auē, what are those shots?*

As the two boats return to the ship, it is quickly established that no one is missing, but the news they bring isn't good.

Cook and the other men had landed unchallenged. The four boys left in charge of the yawl began playing on the beach [as boys do], but were soon being threatened by four armed warriors. One, Te Maro, undeterred by a warning shot from the helmsman of the pinnace, was then fired at and killed. The others dragged his body some way, then left it on the beach.

As a peace-making gesture, Cook left some beads and nails on the body. He noted the warrior's impressive moko. Although carved on the face rather than the buttocks and chest, it was very similar to Tahitian tattooing. They were also physically alike. Was it possible that these two peoples, though separated by thousands of miles of ocean, could be related?

The mood on board the ship that night is grim. And if this first day was bad enough, putting at risk all Cook's plans for friendship and the obtaining of wood and water, the second is worse.

Imagine the fear in the air, the tension. A body still lies on the beach, for it is now seen by the Māori as too sacred for anyone to go near. Cook, Banks and this time Tupaia land and approach the river bank, waiting for the marines to join them. They call out greetings in Tahitian.

On the other side of the river, a hundred or more warriors appear, flourishing their weapons over their heads and dancing what Cook described as their 'War Dance', the terrifying haka. When a warning shot is fired into the water, the haka stops abruptly. And into the eerie silence Tupaia alone calls out in Tahitian.

To the astonishment of everyone on both sides of the river, he is understood. The Māori warriors see a man dressed in similar clothes to the other strangers, but he's darker-skinned and speaks their language! The hopes of Cook and his men must have soared. Now there is a better chance that they can converse, and thereby establish friendship and understanding.

Initially, things improve. Cook asks Tupaia to express friendship, but the locals, remembering yesterday's killing, are unconvinced. After a long conversation, Tupaia persuades a warrior to meet the unarmed Cook on a rock in the river. The two press noses: the traditional Māori greeting of hongi.

Tragically, this is the last moment of goodwill. Twenty or more warriors now surround Cook and the five members of his party, not threatening injury but wanting to trade their weapons for muskets and the gentlemen's swords. Any goodwill vanishes, as Māori try to take swords by force. By the time the warriors retreat, Cook, Banks, Monkhouse and Tupaia have all fired shots. A chief, Te Rakau, lies dead, and two others are wounded in the legs.

Though badly shaken, Cook is determined to find the water and wood that he needs for the ship. His boats cross the bay in search of a likely stream, but he can find no place to land 'on account of the Great Surf which beat everywhere upon the Shore'.

Then, canoes are seen coming in from the sea. He plans to intercept the canoes and take some of the paddlers hostage. On board *Endeavour* he will treat them kindly, win their confidence, and subsequently that of the people ashore.

But despite warning fire over their heads, the Māori paddlers vigorously resist, throwing anchor stones, paddles, even fish. Some — Banks says it is four — are killed, but three young men are taken hostage. Understandably, on board *Endeavour* these youths fear for their lives, but instead find themselves being offered gifts and as much as they can eat of pork, bread and other foods. They tell Tupaia their names and stories of their gods and sing and dance for Cook and the gentlemen.

But no amount of entertainment can lift the hearts of either Cook or Banks. In their cabins that night both write of their guilt and despair that blood has been shed, so contrary to the Earl of Morton's 'Hints' and their own consciences.

'Thus ended the most disagreeable day My life has yet seen, black be the mark for it,' writes Banks, 'and heaven send that such may never return to embitter future reflection.'

The third day in the bay known to the Māori as Tūranganui-a-Kiwa sees no encounters. The sailors put ashore manage to collect some wood, but returning the three youths to their people proves complicated. They have expressed fear of being landed on a part of the bay held by their enemies, and being eaten. [This was the first mention of the indigenous practice of cannibalism.] But they have been able, in another parlay between European and Māori across the river, to state that they have been well treated and that Tupaia is 'almost one of themselves'.

There are still two bodies lying on the riverbank. Eventually an old chief crosses the river with a green bough, evidently a gesture signifying peace. Some gifts are exchanged and a ritual performed. Te Rakau's body is taken away, covered by the red coat one of the young Māori had been given while on board. The body of Te Maro, killed on that terrible first day, remains on the riverbank.

As *Endeavour* prepares to sail at first light the next morning, the three boys are keen to remain aboard. Their local knowledge could be helpful, but Cook is now realising Tupaia's additional value, indispensable as interpreter as well as navigator. Put firmly ashore, despite their qualms, the three boys are observed to be taken across the river in a double-hulled canoe. They seem to be welcomed back.

Endeavour's visit to Tūranganui-a-Kiwa was in most respects a disaster. Given the lack of confrontation with the local people while visiting Tahiti, Cook must have hoped for a similar experience with the inhabitants of this fertile bay, be it an island, or as some on board were convinced, indeed the Great Southern Continent. Given innocence and misunderstandings on both sides, and the importance to Māori of tradition and ritual, the violent clash of cultures was tragic and hardly surprising. But from 9 October onwards, Cook was to develop a genuine interest and appreciation of the people living around the coastline of 'New Zeland'. Six months and many interactions with Māori later, he would describe these indigenous peoples in his journal as a proud race, demanding respect and highly capable — as mariners, boat-builders, gardeners, fishermen and warriors.

With the ship being prepared to sail, there was some small comfort for the botanists, who had managed to collect some forty-odd plants ashore, while artist Sydney Parkinson and Dr Solander's clerk Herbert Spöring [the landscape artist Alexander Buchan, an epileptic, had died back in Tahiti] used the three days confined to the ship to produce some fine sketches of the landscape.

And between his visits ashore, Cook got out a sheet of sturdy paper and began to draw the rough outline of the bay and Young Nick's Head. It marked the beginning of his great New Zealand chart.

Because the bay of Tūranganui-a-Kiwa, apparently so fertile, had disappointingly 'afforded us no one thing we wanted', he regretfully put aside his intention of calling it Endeavour Bay. On the beginnings of his chart he wrote instead, Poverty Bay.

The red jacket, probably a marine's and gifted to one of the Māori youths who spent a night aboard *Endeavour*, laid over the fallen warrior Te Rakau. Anthropologist Anne Salmond writes that the garment became a prized heirloom known as Te Makura and was worn by chiefs into battle.

BARRIER ISLES

Pt Charles

CAPE COLVIL

RIVER THAMES

MERCURY POINT

Mercury Isles

MERCURY BAY Var. 11.9 E.

Court of Aldermen

N

H

E

I

Z

The Mayor

BAY OF PL

Flat Island

Woody Head

Town
Many Fortified Towns
Low Land Point
Low Land Bay

Albetross Point

Mount Edgcumbe

4

To Cape Turnagain

Now, leaving Poverty Bay, Cook began his survey in earnest, spending many hours a day taking the measurements required, absorbing information from the linesmen and lookouts, and slowly extending the coastline's important features on the chart.

Off Newfoundland, he had used the 'triangulated survey', but this method was time-consuming and required the surveyor to go ashore to create a base line for further sightings and calculations. More suitable for New Zealand was the time-honoured 'running survey', hardly changed for centuries.

This system involved taking frequent bearings and horizontal angles of prominent landmarks, then plotting them — while also sounding continually with the lead for the depth and nature of the seabed, and measuring the distance run between observations with the ship's rudimentary wooden log towed astern.

For accuracy, many factors were involved: knowing the ship's speed and direction; the frequency of the bearings and angles taken with the magnetic compass; the exactness of the astronomical observations measured with the sextant; any knowledge of the tides and currents; and of course, the weather.

Mariners under sail were often frustrated. Bad weather usually drove a ship out to sea; fine weather enabled a surveyor to get closer to land for better measurements but also put his ship at risk. Sometimes, weighing up any threat to personal safety, he or his officers might take the theodolite and azimuth compass ashore to make observations from a suitable hilltop.

Cook's running survey depended on continual observations, constant vigilance and great perseverance; and above all, on his ability to combine basic information about the ship's movement with clues offered by the coast and the sea.

As *Endeavour* sailed south from Poverty Bay, Cook must have been wondering how the success of his survey would be affected by what he'd already learned of Māori curiosity, defiance and belligerence. But for now, he was about to learn much more about their sea-going traditions — the fine canoes they built and could handle with such skill.

The calm conditions of the next afternoon were perfect for canoes to put to sea and investigate more closely this strange vessel with its cloud-like sails. As *Endeavour* lay barely

Late eighteenth-century navigators had only basic instruments to establish depths, speed and position. The lead [top], thrown into the water by a linesman, established depths of water below the keel. The log, a knotted rope [middle], attached to a wooden float, measured a ship's speed [hence today's term, knots]. The sextant [bottom], used to calculate latitude, was invented in 1759. Although largely replaced in the late twentieth century by GPS and other electronic aids to navigation, sextants are still being manufactured and used, specially by small boat sailors.

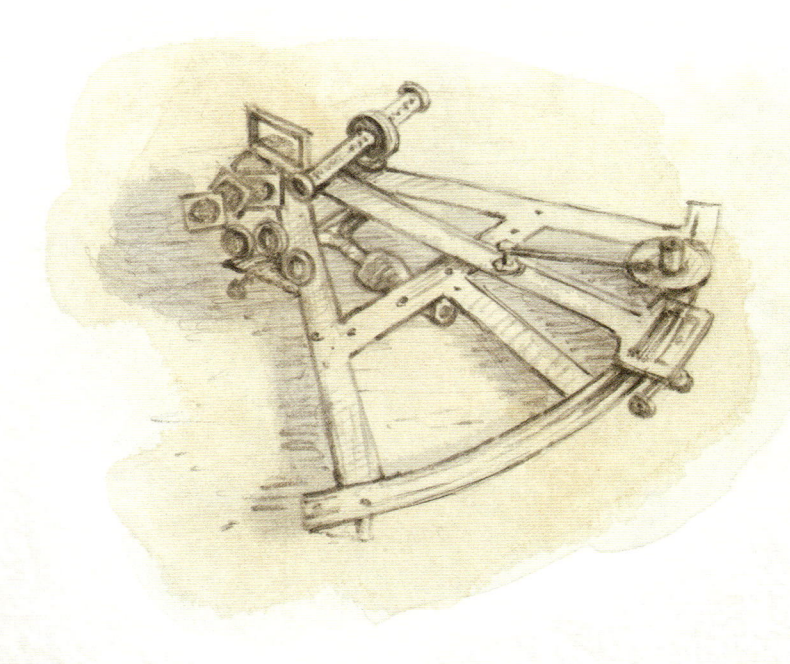

moving, several canoes approached. One came alongside; Cook wondered whether the paddlers had heard of his kind treatment of the three Tūranganui-a-Kiwa boys entertained on board two days earlier.

These intrepid canoeists encouraged others to come alongside, and soon a number of the paddlers were aboard *Endeavour*. Two hours of lively trading with the sailors followed. One group, having traded away most of their paddles, offered to sell the canoe!

On the canoes' departure, it was found three paddlers had quite happily remained on board. Later, however, two more canoes approached. Cook writes that the Māori in the canoes needed reassurance that 'we did not Eat men,' before they could be enticed to come alongside and take the three paddlers ashore. 'It should seem,' he writes, 'that these people have such a Custom among them.'

If Cook now hoped for improved relationships, he was too optimistic. Coaxing *Endeavour* in light airs around the southern tip of the small island he called Portland, he was disconcerted by four canoes 'full of People' which approached and were brought close in under the stern. Only after warning shots were fired did the clearly hostile paddlers retire.

This was just the prelude to the next day, when *Endeavour* looked for an anchorage in the 'great Bay' that Cook would call after First Lord of the Admiralty, Edward Hawke. Two ship's boats, nearly ready to go ashore for wood and water, were hastily hauled back aboard when five large canoes were seen approaching, richly carved and decorated with feather streamers. The paddlers wore greenstone ornaments and carried taiaha [pikes].

Cook estimated these canoes each carried between eighty and ninety men. Despite European overtures of friendship, they seemed 'fully bent on attacking us'. Eventually, warnings from Tupaia and the four-pound cannon persuaded them to withdraw, though one canoe returned later for some friendlier conversation and trading with Tupaia.

The next day confirmed that this bay was fertile and its people prosperous. Early in the morning some fishing canoes came alongside. Cook, anxious for amicable trading, bought some fish, despite that it was 'stinking' — probably dried fish and perfectly edible. But trouble came with a second and larger canoe, manned by twenty-two men, one wearing a cloak of a black fur. Cook offered cloth, which was taken, but the fur cape [probably dogskin] was not traded in return before the canoe was paddled away from the ship.

This second encounter had a tragic ending. With some canoes still circling the ship, and Tupaia's boy Taiata watching from a perch over *Endeavour*'s side, some paddlers pulled him down into their canoe. To prevent the boy being carried away, Cook ordered shots to be fired near the canoe. Unhurt, Taiata jumped into the sea and swam for his life to a boat lowered from *Endeavour*.

'For this daring attempt,' wrote Cook grimly that night, 'two or three Māori paid with the loss of their lives.' Indeed, 'many more would have suffer'd had it not been for fear of killing the Boy.' Taiata had become a favourite of the sailors on board, and Cook had sons of his own back in Mile End. To mark the incident, he named the spectacular headland off to starboard, 'Cape Kidnapper'.

His chart now showed the great curving sweep of Hawke's Bay, with the tacks he had made to get *Endeavour* close to the shore, and the depths of water along his course.

In his journals he was adding increasingly detailed descriptions of coastal features and signs of habitation. Probably he was shown the wonderfully detailed sketches of large canoes and their defiant paddlers being produced by Parkinson and Spöring. He knew that on their return to England these visual records would all be valuable.

But as *Endeavour* passed the high white cliffs of Cape Kidnapper, Cook must have been a deeply worried man.

It was now clear that the Māori, on land and equally on the water, were not going to make it easy for him to replenish vital wood, greens and water as they worked their way around the coast — however extensive that coast turned out to be.

How far would he have to keep *Endeavour* offshore — not only for the ship's navigational safety but also out of reach of attack? Was this continual threat of aggression going to prevent any proper chart being completed?

Even if Cook was sceptical, many on board [especially Banks] still firmly believed that they were sailing along the coast of the Great Southern Continent.

As *Endeavour* anchored in bays on the North Island's eastern coasts, Cook and his crew became familiar with canoes putting out from the shore to encircle the ship, sometimes more than forty at a time.

41

For another day *Endeavour* continued south, passing more white cliffs, and villages on the tops and sides of hills as well as in the valleys. They noted cooking fires, and spring snow still clinging to the higher ridges inland. But with no sign of a harbour, and the coastline 'visibly altering for the worse', Cook decided on 17 October that turning north would bring 'a greater Probability of success'.

A few miles south of 40 degrees latitude, he tacked the ship and stood to the north. That high bluff now on his port side — obviously, he would call that Cape Turnagain.

For the first time since landfall nearly two weeks earlier, *Endeavour* was lashed by fresh westerly gales as she plunged on north towards the Isle of Portland. Lightning flashed across the dark skies. The heavy weather could not have helped Cook's low spirits, but visits from the shore during the next two days were encouraging: first, five local people who accepted gifts and food, before insisting they stay on board for the night, and the next day, further inspection by canoes, and one man who came aboard.

Joseph Banks and Dr Solander returned from the *Endeavour* voyage with 30,000 plant specimens, some preserved between the pages of John Milton's epic poem *Paradise Lost*. The book is among the Banks collection at the Natural History Museum, London.

All seemed friendly enough. Perhaps, Cook mused, their confidence, curiosity and gratitude could be explained by reports of friendly treatment offered to others who'd earlier visited the ship? Perhaps the tide had turned?

With Poverty Bay dropping astern, *Endeavour* was again coasting along unfamiliar countryside. They could see luxuriant forests, villages and cultivated land. Two sheltered bays looked inviting, so on 21 October Cook cautiously brought *Endeavour* to anchor in Anaura Bay, noted on the chart as 'Tegadoo' [curiously, among all the Anglo names; biographer J.C. Beaglehole suggests 'tegadoo' was Cook's rendering of 'te ngaru', the Māori words for the sound of surf breaking in the bay]. A landing here would be their first ashore in ten days.

The initial contacts were encouraging. Two high-ranking and heavily tattooed chiefs came aboard and were reassured by Tupaia that the ship came in peace, seeking water. The next day saw some friendly trading, with the Māori offering sweet potatoes and wild 'sellery'. There was also some contact with the women, and the chance for Banks and Solander to 'botanise'.

But Anaura Bay's surf made loading the heavy water casks onto the small boats very difficult, so *Endeavour* put to sea and was guided by locals to a bay a few miles along the coast. At Uawa [now Tolaga] Bay, the visitors were told they would find water.

Here *Endeavour* spent five useful and trouble-free days. There was some good-humoured trading of fish for cloth, bottles and beads. Parties ashore picked great quantities of wild 'sellery', the New Zealand variety known to Māori as pūhā, and filled many casks of water and boatloads of wood. They tried dredging for shellfish, without much success, but found a native tree, probably mānuka, from which fine brooms for cleaning the ship could be made. The armourer was able to light a fire to repair the iron tiller braces. Banks and Solander happily collected specimens and shot birds and at Banks' suggestion, Spöring produced a fine sketch of a spectacular natural archway of coastal rock, with a fortified stronghold on its span.

With the natives giving 'not the least disturbance' and his men usefully employed ashore, Cook and the astronomer Charles Green were able to spend a morning taking observations of the sun and moon. These established to their satisfaction the bay's longitude from the Meridian of Greenwich and its exact latitude.

Many hours were also spent recording his observations of the inhabitants' life and culture: their religion, suggestions of cannibalism, their decorative arts like carving and the powerful origin stories later to be known as the traditions of Rangi and Papa. Tupaia's long conversations with the local priests probably provided much of the information, but Cook was also an astute observer. During long walks into the hills, he noted the different species of trees, many beautiful birds and the lack of four-footed animals either tame or wild [except dogs and the native rat, both eaten by Māori].

With sufficient wood, water and greens aboard, on 29 October *Endeavour* weighed anchor. Two days later she rounded the point which Cook was so confident would be the 'Eastermost land on this whole coast' that he named it East Cape.

But any hopes of continuing friendly relations were soon dashed. Two days along the coast, *Endeavour* was approached by five canoes, one large enough to hold forty paddlers 'all armed with pikes &c', challenging the ship with chanting and haka. Two rounds of warning shots saw them paddling so speedily back to shore that Cook wrote on his chart, 'Cape Runaway'.

Day after day, canoes put out from the shore to inspect and challenge the visitor. On 1 November, Cook noted the astonishing number of some forty to fifty canoes along the shores. Several came to visit, and traded fresh lobsters, mussels and eels; a different group took offerings of linen but gave nothing in return, so they too were frightened away by musket and four-pounder cannon shot, fired wide. On two days running, a large double-hulled sailing canoe came close enough for the paddlers to pelt the ship with stones, and for Spöring to produce the now-famous sketch, now held in the British Library, which powerfully captured the mood of defiance and the grandeur of the craft.

The next day pikes were hurled at *Endeavour* from three more circling canoes. On 4 November there were three visits. The first came with three canoes, each impressively hewn from a single large tree and manned by 'mostly naked' paddlers, who again hurled pikes.

The second was a group of canoes that accompanied the ship to anchor and before leaving at nightfall threatened to attack the next morning. Twice during the night some returned, only to retire when they realised that not all *Endeavour*'s hands were asleep.

The third visit, more alarming still, was also made after *Endeavour* was anchored off what is now known as Cook's Beach, Whitianga. Canoes approached 'from all parts of the bay', manned by some 130 or 140 armed men, apparently intent on attacking the ship. They hung about for nearly three hours, sometimes 'Trading' and sometimes 'Tricking', and eventually retired. But it had taken warning musket shots and 'one great gun' [none fired to cause harm, though a ball did go through the hull of one canoe] to demonstrate the ship's firepower.

So why did Cook decide to anchor here, putting his ship and the lives of his men at considerable risk? Crossing the stretch of sea he named Bay of Plenty, he'd been impressed by the luxuriant nature of the countryside, the extent of cultivated lands, the villages and marae built on hilltops and fortified by palisades, banks and ditches. The large number of canoes pulled up on the beaches was a sign of prosperous communities.

His chart was now showing 'Mowtohara' [Whale Island, off modern-day Whakatane] and inland, Mount Edgecumbe [possibly after his sergeant]. Islands noted were tiny Flat Island [off Tauranga] and further out, White Island [an active volcano, but apparently quiet at the time]. To the north were the Mayor and the cluster of steep rocks he called, in a rare flash of wry humour, The Court of Aldermen.

The dominant figure among the many Māori shown in Sydney Parkinson's dramatic depiction of a waka taua [war canoe] is this cloaked chief. [After Sydney Parkinson's 'New Zealand War Canoe Bidding Defiance to the Ship', 1769]

Charting a safe passage through these islands and along the mainland's craggy coastline was just what Cook relished. But he knew from the last few days there were considerable numbers of Māori living along these fertile coasts. Could their defiance and aggression easily turn deadly, or were the hurling of stones, paddles and pikes and the aggressive haka some sort of warrior ritual?

He could have continued north, charting as he went, but still with no idea whether it was the coastline of an island or a continent, or of its relationship to Tasman's 1642 coastline somewhere out to the west.

It was Cook the surveyor who made the decision, over Cook the cautious ship's captain.

Only five days hence, on the afternoon of Thursday 9 November, the planet Mercury would pass over the face of the sun. Cook needed a good harbour and convenient place ashore to observe this accurately. 'It will be wholy Visible here if the day is clear. If we be so fortunate … the Longitude of this place and Country will thereby be very accurately determined.'

Endeavour spent eleven days at Mercury Bay. Cook clearly felt confident enough to order the ship to be heeled, allowing both sides of the hull to be scrubbed. He kept the men busy — fishing with the net, dredging for shellfish, again with not much success. Parties went ashore to cut wood, collect water and the wild 'sellery' that the one-handed cook John Thompson served daily. The officers also tried fishing, or were sent off in the boats to sound the depths of water for Cook's large-scale chart of the bay and river. Women and children helped Banks and Solander gather plants and rocks.

On 9 November, in clear weather, Cook and astronomer Charles Green duly went ashore with their instruments to a sandy beach not far from the ship to carry out their observations.

Up till this point, interaction with the local inhabitants had been friendly, trading welcome supplies of fish for cloth and nails.

The carvings on prow and stern of the waka taua [war canoes] fascinated artists Parkinson and Spöring. Joseph Banks records that while in Tolaga Bay a party went ashore on an island and saw the largest canoe yet encountered: 68 feet [nearly 21 metres] long, built from three tree trunks, its head 'richly carved in their fashion'. Spöring must have spent many hours on the beach, capturing the intricate details in close-up.
[After Herman Spöring, 'The Head of a Canoe', 1769.]

While Cook was away, five strange canoes approached the ship, two large and three small, adding their presence to others already alongside. The newcomers were armed and maybe hostile, but settled into some brisk trading. With their carved canoes and fine cloaks they appeared to the sailors to be better off than the poorer locals.

Before he was able to return to the ship, Cook heard a shot. Then came a loud BOOM from the four-pound gun that sent all the canoes scurrying off.

Back on board, Cook was furious to hear that the officer left in charge, Lieutenant Gore, had fired the shot and killed a paddler. Gore had passed down some cloth in exchange for the man's dogskin cloak, but received nothing back.

Incensed by shouts of triumph from the departing canoe, Gore raised his musket. This punishment Cook regarded as too severe, since they'd learned enough about the people to know how to deal with 'Trifling faults' like this without taking away their lives. [Tupaia perhaps had explained to Cook that for Māori, exchange of gifts could be delayed, unlike the British who expected the transaction to be fairly completed right then and there.]

The incident worsened the relationship between Cook and his second-in-command, already cool. Both must have been hugely relieved that during their final days in Whitianga, there were no repercussions from the killing.

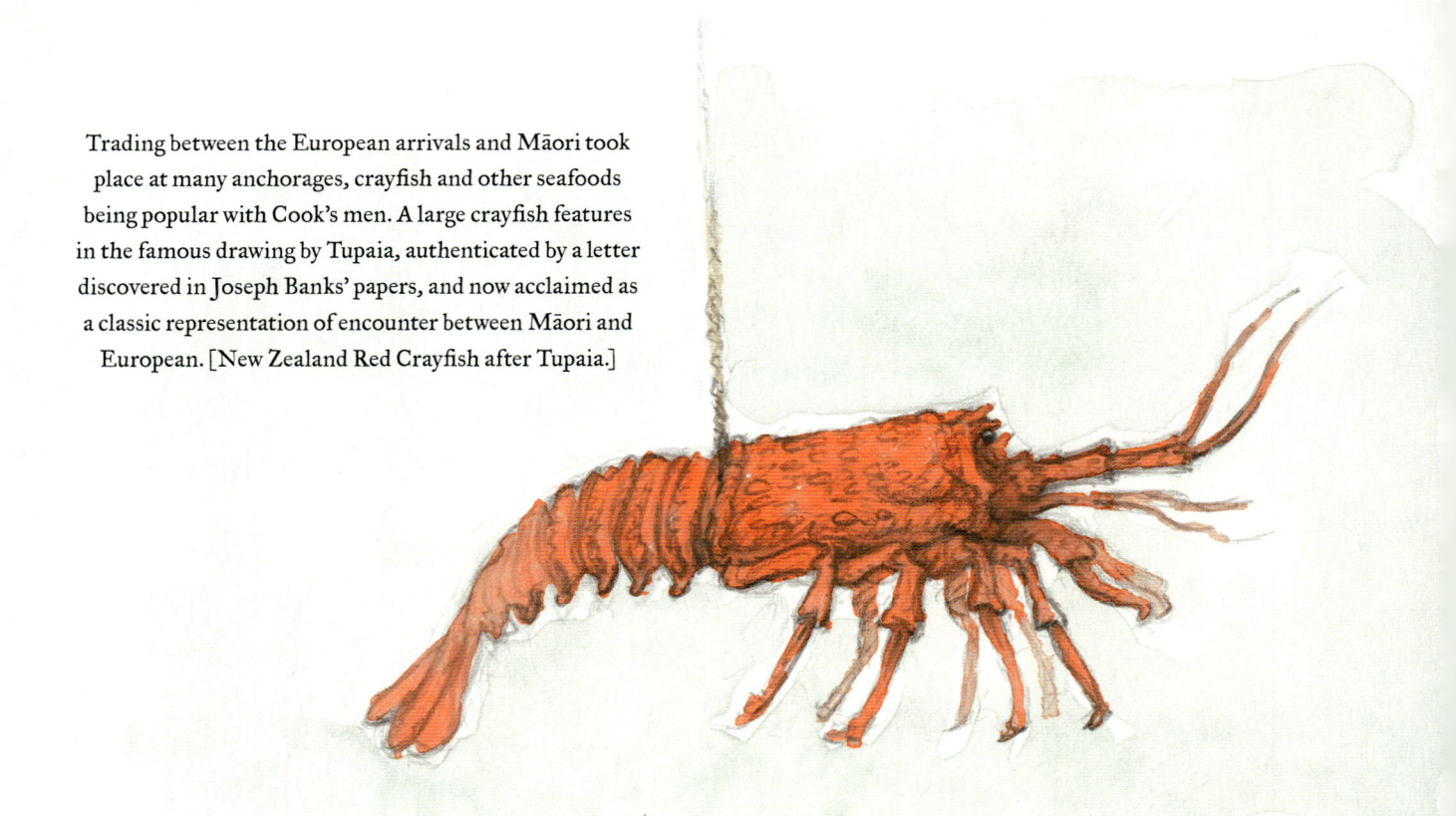

Trading between the European arrivals and Māori took place at many anchorages, crayfish and other seafoods being popular with Cook's men. A large crayfish features in the famous drawing by Tupaia, authenticated by a letter discovered in Joseph Banks' papers, and now acclaimed as a classic representation of encounter between Māori and European. [New Zealand Red Crayfish after Tupaia.]

On 12 November, Cook went off overnight with Banks and his team to explore four or five miles up the river at the head of the bay [Mangrove River on his chart]. He climbed enough hills to report that, with no cultivation to be seen anywhere, these local people lived on seafoods [notably oysters and enormous crayfish] and fern-root, which they roasted, pounded and made into a sort of bread. And with no houses visible anywhere, Cook decided they must sleep under trees and small temporary shades.

Cook's final expedition was with Banks and Solander to the northern side of Mercury Bay. They were received hospitably and shown around the two pā in the area. At the larger one, they admired the extensive fortifications and different kinds of weapons. Two young warriors staged a mock battle for the visitors.

For *Endeavour*, this visit to Mercury Bay had been the least troublesome so far. A boy of about twelve, Horeta Te Taniwha, was welcomed on board the ship and his recollections of that visit were recorded many decades later. He spoke of the old men believing the ship to be an atua, a god, and its people not human beings but tupua, or 'goblins'. Watching the ship's boats being rowed ashore, the old men said these goblins must have their eyes at the back of their heads: 'they pull on shore with their backs to the land to which they are going!'

Initially frightened away, the children came back and wondered at the visitors' white skins and blue eyes. With no common language, 'we laughed, and these goblins also laughed, so we were pleased'. And they identified one 'supreme man' in the ship by his gentlemanly and noble manner, a man who seldom spoke but asked one of the chiefs to draw on the deck in charcoal a chart of the islands to the north. To explain Te Rerenga Wairua [Cape Reinga] in the far north of the island, where the spirits depart for the underworld, the old man lay down as if dead. Te Taniwha's account relates that the Europeans remained mystified, but as a gesture of goodwill Cook handed the chief some seed potatoes which later produced good crops in the area.

Two tasks remained for Cook before leaving Mercury Bay. One was the formality required of him, to cut *Endeavour*'s name and date on a tree near the watering place and raise the Union flag, 'taking possession' of the site in the name of King George III.

The second was to land on one of the tiny islands guarding the bay. From its summit he hoped to spot any sunken rocks or other dangers to be avoided on departure. There was a large swell running after a day of fresh gales, and he would not sail until he judged it safe.

The morning of 15 November was clear with a light westerly. Leaving the bay, Cook took *Endeavour* east of the two Mercury Islands, and once more into the open sea.

Cook's men were regularly sent ashore, where local Māori sometimes showed them where to gather edible green 'sellery' [to Māori, pūhā], which was served to the crew and officers alike in soups as a preventative against scurvy. Leaves from rimu and mānuka were also collected, to be mixed with molasses and malt extract to make 'spruce beer' for thirsty crew. Mānuka is still called by Cook's given name of 'tea tree'.

NORTH CAPE
DIEMEN
SANDY BAY
Var.12.42 E
Mount Camel
Knuckle point
Doubtless Bay
Bay Point
Cavalle head
Cavalle Isles
POINT POCOC
BAY OF ISLANDS
Piercy Isle
CAPE BRETT
Poor Knight
Bushey Point
Bream head
Hen and Chic
BREAM BAY
Bream Tale
POINT RODNEY
FALSE BAY

5

Among Islands

Until now, from their landfall five weeks earlier, *Endeavour* had been sailing along a clearly defined coastline with relatively few offshore islands.

Now, and until she cleared the Bay of Islands some 300 km [186 miles] further north, *Endeavour* would nearly always be within sight of land, either mainland or the many islands of the Hauraki Gulf and the Bay of Islands. Deciding which was which required the constant taking of sights and hours of careful observation.

Charting this section of the North Island would pose Cook extra challenges, involving much thought and discussion with his officers before outlines could confidently be added to the chart. True, the winds were mostly from the southwest or south, helpful for a square-rigger on a northerly course, but there were the ever-present risks, by day and especially at night, posed by hidden reefs, isolated rocks, and fast-flowing tidal streams which could swiftly carry a ship into danger.

For the first two days from Mercury Bay, fresh gales and heavy squalls drove *Endeavour* well out to sea. Turning back to the land, but still unsure whether it was mainland or islands, Cook rounded a prominent point he named Cape Colvill [after Lord Colvill, a captain from his Canadian days].

Soon, with land on both sides and in 'whistling light Airs all round the Compass', he decided that *Endeavour* must be at the entrance of a strait, bay or river.

The light winds and the steadily decreasing depths of water shouted by the linesman made him extra cautious. Unusually, he anchored overnight, rather than run further in the dark and find the ship aground on the muddy bottom. The next day, after an easy sail of about twenty miles due south, he dropped anchor nine miles from the mouth of a river 'as broad as the Thames River at Greenwich'. And 'River Thames' was what he named the whole of the deep inlet now known as the Firth of Thames.

With *Endeavour* safely anchored and local Māori friendly, Cook decided that this presented a good opportunity to see something of the interior. Although the previous day two canoes had thrown stones at the ship before a musket shot scared them off, a second visit by three large canoes had been cordial. Some paddlers had come aboard the ship without

Cook explored '12 or 14' miles up the broad, tree-lined Waihou River, which he named after the River Thames. Banks noted the river plains on both sides being 'completely cloathd with the finest timber my Eyes ever beheld … every tree as straight as a pine and of immense size: still the higher we came the more numerous they were'.

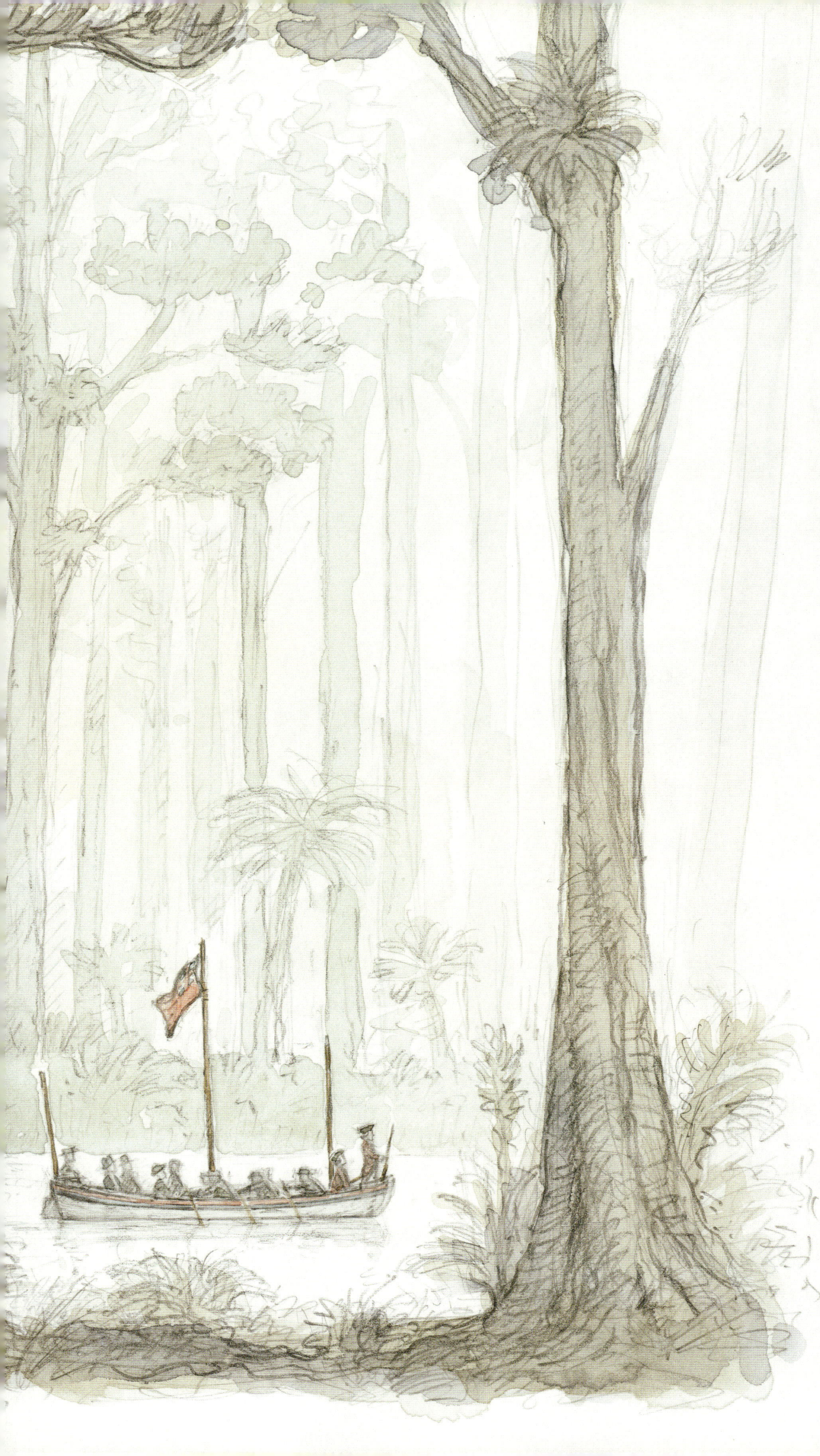

The cat o' nine tails, widely used in the Royal Navy for punishing miscreant seamen, was rarely employed on Cook's first voyage. Made up of nine plaited thongs of cotton cord up to a metre long, it was designed to break the skin and cause intense pain. Twelve lashes, perhaps for theft or drunkenness, were considered relatively light; a flogging of 200 lashes was not unknown if the man had not died first.

hesitation, greeted Tupaia by name, and received small gifts. Probably, Cook thought, favourable news had preceded them up the coast.

So, at daybreak on 20 November, Cook, Banks, Solander and Tupaia took the pinnace and longboat and went exploring up the broad and meandering Waihou River. This was Cook's longest inland excursion of any of his visits to New Zealand. Three miles up, the tidal salt water gave way to fresh. A little further on, the party was warmly welcomed at a fortified village.

By noon, the river was winding between magnificent stands of kahikatea [white pine]. Cook was hugely impressed by these ancient giants, all unknown species. With his quadrant, he calculated the height of one massive trunk, up to the first branch, as 89 feet [27 metres], and its girth fully 19 feet 6 inches [nearly 6 metres].

The expedition up the river came at a cost. Back at the river mouth, faced with adverse winds and incoming flood tide, Cook and party had no choice but to spend a wet and unpleasant night at anchor in the two small boats. And when they finally reached *Endeavour* the next morning, it was blowing so hard that he ordered the sailors to put out more anchor cable and lower the heavy wooden topgallant yards onto the deck, to reduce windage. Dragging anchor in this enclosed and shallow bay could only end in catastrophe.

The Thames area visit, so far without incident, ended unhappily. Playing it safe as *Endeavour* made slow progress northwards, Cook twice brought the ship to anchor. Waiting for the tide to turn, he and Solander went ashore, leaving Lieutenant Hickes as commanding officer while some brisk trading took place between the sailors and some local people who'd come on board.

On return, he was dismayed to find that there'd been a flogging — not of a sailor, but a local warrior caught stealing a sand-filled 'half-minute glass' from the binnacle. This instrument was used with the log line to determine the ship's speed, crucial for navigation. The theft was serious enough for Hickes to order twelve lashes with a 'Catt of nine Tails'. Tupaia reassured

The half-minute glass, mounted on the binnacle or stand in front of the helmsman, was used in conjunction with a ship's log for keeping track of distance travelled. Time, usually an interval of an hour, was accurately measured by sand, water or mercury dropping from an upper to a lower glass compartment through a small aperture.

In unfamiliar coastal waters, Cook relied heavily on his linesman 'throwing the line' to call out the depths. A heavy piece of lead was attached to a long rope, some 20 fathoms [120 feet, 36.6 metres] for shallow waters, or 100 fathoms [600 feet, 182.8 metres] in deeper waters. It was lowered until touching bottom; leather 'marks' indicated depths in fathoms [6 feet, 1.8 metres].

the watching Māori that the man was only to be beaten, not killed. Back in his canoe, the man was further beaten by an old chief, possibly his father. Apparently the punishment was seen as justified; the shame, the British were learning, was not so much in the stealing as being caught.

After weighing anchor on 23 November, *Endeavour* spent the next four days running up the coast of the sheltered area to become known as the Hauraki Gulf. [The Māori name invokes its frequent northerly winds.]

With land now visible on every side of the ship, Cook's journals make it clear that he was taking ever more frequent sights to determine latitude. Also, that the linesman was being kept very busy, heaving his lead and calling out the depths of water.

There is good reason why the stretch of coast and the offshore islands from Waiheke Island north to Point Rodney are disappointingly sketchy or incomplete on Cook's chart. Squally weather, with thunder, lightning, torrential rain and winds strong enough to order double reefs in the topsails — all demanded the most cautious navigation and skilled seamanship. Several times Cook noted that the weather, even when it moderated, frustrated his hopes of investigating the coastline more fully.

He was able to chart the eastern coast of Waiheke Island [spending a night at anchor off the north-eastern tip of the island], along with parts of Ponui and Rangitoto islands. These inner Gulf islands, he decided, formed the Barrier Isles, 'a Chain of Large and Small Islands' that very likely defended some good harbours from the sea, especially on the western shore.

How right he was — seventy years later, the first governor of the infant colony of New Zealand, Captain William Hobson, would choose the Waitematā Harbour on the western shore of the Gulf as the site for a capital city to be named Auckland.

Few canoes visited *Endeavour* as she ran north before typically fresh Hauraki southwesterlies. Those that did were large and well-built craft, their paddlers covered from head to foot with a body paint of red ochre and oil — something, Cook noted, the Europeans had not seen before.

Spotting a wide bay just south of a broad river mouth, Cook decided to anchor for the night. The waters around the ship were teeming with fish, and within a very short time the sailors had caught nearly a hundred. Cook called them bream [probably tarakihi] and wrote Bream Bay on the chart. It was a spectacular anchorage, dominated by the towering peaks of the Whangarei Heads. Not far offshore were the craggy islands that Cook noted as the Hen and Chickens and further north, the curiously named Poor Knights.

At night, inland fires were proof of villages, though no canoes came calling until dusk the next day — 26 November — when *Endeavour* was coasting along in light airs about four miles from land. The ship was approached by seven canoes carrying about two hundred Māori, many elaborately tattooed, and including some women.

The paddlers told Tupaia they had heard tell of *Endeavour*. He persuaded some to climb aboard the ship, and Cook presented two, apparently chiefs, with gifts. Some trading took place, but with little goodwill evident; back in their canoes, the paddlers threw stones and shook their spears. The warning musket fire, followed by a four-pound shot, frightened the visitors sufficiently to break off their haka and send the canoes speedily back to shore.

Cook was not to know, of course, that *Endeavour* was approaching one of the most intensely populated areas of either Aeheinomouwe or Tovypoenammu; indeed one of the very earliest sites of Polynesian settlement on the two islands. The latest encounter had not been encouraging, especially as the news of their presence on the coast had clearly preceded them.

As he tossed on his hard suspended cot, and heard the bells mark the four-hourly change of the night watch, Cook must have wondered how far his good intentions and luck would hold.

At dawn on 27 November, several canoes put off from the shore, followed by others. One, fully seventy feet long, was finely carved and its people wore dogskin cloaks and carried weapons of stone and whalebone. Cook estimated that by noon a 'good many' had come on board, with another 170 in canoes alongside. Though friendly enough, these Māori would not trade, and left without incident.

The gentle easterlies had now carried *Endeavour* abreast of a high point of land, which he named Cape Brett for Rear-Admiral Sir Piercy Brett. Not far offshore lay a small high island with a hole 'pierced thro' it like the Arch of a Bridge'. This provided a nice little pun, thus Piercy Isle [today's famous 'Hole in the Rock'].

The clear summer day brought strong proof that this area was densely populated and prosperous. Over the previous twenty-four hours Cook estimated 'not less than 400 or 500' Māori had come alongside or climbed on board the slowly moving ship. These people were stout, well-built and well-dressed, not many with facial tattoos but some with tattooed buttocks and thighs, similar to the Tahitians.

Again, the day passed without incident. But the next day, almost becalmed off the islands Cook called the Cavalle Isles [now the Cavalli Islands], *Endeavour* was approached by several canoes to trade fish. Despite all Tupaia's efforts, the paddlers became aggressive, hurling stones and fish at the ship and directly at Cook himself. His musket fire in angry retaliation wounded one or more paddlers, and sent the canoes back to shore. Very likely troubled by losing his temper and causing harm, contrary to all he believed in, Cook stood *Endeavour* out to sea for the night.

Tomorrow, however, regardless of danger, he would turn *Endeavour* back to the mainland, into the 'large and pretty deep bay' already noted and which he was determined to explore.

Any Māori looking out to sea on 28 November 1770 cannot help but notice *Endeavour* approaching the coast in all her square-rigged magnificence. Beating to windward in a fresh westerly, 'right in our teeth', Cook has crowded on all the sail he can.

Even so, it takes the best part of two days to reach the entrance to the bay and drop anchor under the lee of Motuarohia Island [Roberton Island]. Cook the perfectionist cartographer gazes at the green islands around him, many inhabited, and wonders how much surveying he will be permitted to do. Will sending off his crew in small boats to explore this beautiful bay, even with the marines in attendance, be just asking for trouble?

Their first day could have ended very badly. Soon after anchoring, *Endeavour* is surrounded by about thirty-five canoes, holding perhaps 400 people. The usual courtesies are followed: chiefs are invited on board and presented with gifts.

All goes well until the sailors spy paddlers from several canoes trying to tow away *Endeavour*'s anchor buoy, vital for the ship's safety when at anchor. The marines' musket fire wounds one paddler, and only the great gun, fired over their heads, prompts them to relinquish the buoy and convinces most of the canoes to disperse. Yet, encouragingly, Tupaia persuades some to return.

After dinner, Cook — rashly, as it turns out — decides to go ashore on the island, taking Banks, Solander and the marines. All are armed. Their two small boats are not followed by the canoes still circling the ship, which Cook thinks is a good sign.

However, once landed on the beach, they become aware of canoes being paddled at great speed toward them. Suddenly Cook and his party find themselves surrounded by maybe 300 armed warriors. The situation is now perilous: Cook has drawn a line in the sand, but the warriors have begun a vigorous haka, while other Māori are trying to seize the boats pulled up on shore. Cook, Banks and Solander warn off Māori advances with smallshot fired from their muskets; Cook coolly recalls in his journal the warriors 'only seem'd to want some one of resolution to head them'. Despite their far greater numbers, the warriors do not yet press their advantage, while Cook tries to restrain his party from firing fatal shots. Of the hundreds on the beach, no Europeans and 'only one or 2 of them was Hurt with small Shott, for I avoided killing any one of them as much as Possible, and for that reason withheld our people from firing'. The skirmish ends when Lieutenant Hickes, watching from the ship, realises his captain is in deep trouble. He quickly orders the big guns brought to bear for a cannonade of four-pounder shots to be fired over all their heads. The thunderous noise and smoke are enough to send the warriors back to their canoes and diffuse the situation.

Cook's journal indicates that after this frightening experience he decides to cut his losses; early the next morning he puts to sea. He'd earlier climbed the sharply pointed peak of Motuarohia to see as much as he could of the bay, and both boats had been loaded up with wild 'sellery'. Some of the island's inhabitants had, since the fracas on the beach, treated his party kindly. It is a good note on which to leave.

Before dawn, the anchor is raised, but with insufficient wind for a safe passage between the islands, Cook is forced to anchor again. Still shaken by the previous day's events, he is in no mood to be lenient with three crew members who left their duty when ashore the previous night and stole sweet potatoes from a Māori plantation. Each receives a dozen lashes and one,

Following the first-day encounter with local Māori, the island of Motuarohia offered Cook a good anchorage from which to explore the heavily populated Bay of Islands. On its steep eastern point a palisaded pā provided a spectacular lookout over the bay and the mainland coastline. Cook climbed the summits of both Motuarohia and nearby Moturua island. [After an unsigned sketch, probably by Sydney Parkinson.]

Matthew Cox, earns himself an extra six and confinement below decks when he insists he has done no wrong. His captain, determined to be seen by all as fair in dealings with crew and locals alike, thinks otherwise.

Contrary northerlies keep *Endeavour* at anchor for the next four days. With no further challenges from the locals, Cook and his men make good use of the time. The officers go off in the small boats to take soundings for a large-scale chart of the bay, right up as far as today's Tapeka Point. Men are sent ashore to ensure all the water barrels are filled, and to gather vast quantities of 'sellery' and grass for the ship's sheep, all in preparation for whatever lay ahead.

Others go fishing with the nets, not very successfully. Local fishermen, they discover, use far bigger and more effective nets made of green flax — some a thousand yards long — to catch an abundance of fish, which they are happy to trade. Cook notes sharks and stingrays in among those he gives English names of mullet, bream and mackerel; many are a good deal bigger than similar fish in English waters.

On board, Parkinson and Spöring spend the days drawing wonderfully accurate sketches of the landscape and settlements, including a spectacular fortified village perched above the steep eastern slopes of Motuarohia.

Cook himself goes with Banks and Solander to explore more islands and the southern shore of the mainland. They note the area's obvious fertility, the thriving cultivations of yams, kumara and taro, and the villages built on naturally secure sites. Cook notes that 'the inhabitants of this Bay are far more numerous than at any other place we have yet been in and seem to live in friendship one with another, although it doth not at all appear that they are united under one head.'

At last, on 5 December, a brisk southwesterly comes in, and during the night *Endeavour* puts to sea. Cook writes ruefully that he's not made an accurate survey of the bay, having insufficient time to do it properly. He is however confident that he's seen enough to know that the bay itself offers good anchorages and 'every kind of refreshment for Shipping'.

Māori call the bay Tokerau; on his chart Cook, reminded of his visit to a similar bay on the west coast of Newfoundland two years earlier, writes Bay of Islands.

Woody Head

Gannet Isle

Albetross Point

Sugar-loaf Isles

Sugar-loaf Point

CAPE EGMONT

Mount Egmont

6

Contrary Winds

Endeavour had now been following the eastern coastline of the upper northern island for eight weeks. In a few places, moderate surf had made landing difficult, but most beaches were sandy and relatively benign. They'd sailed as close as Cook dared, but struck no reefs. The prevailing winds were south-westerlies or southerlies, thus offshore. No gales had yet been severe or adverse enough to drive *Endeavour* hundreds of miles out to sea.

All this was about to change for the worse, even before *Endeavour* had cleared the Bay of Islands.

The fair wind that had prompted Cook to weigh anchor at dawn lasted only a few hours. During the day, the sailors caught more than a hundred fish. Canoes warily circled the ship as she made little or no headway towards the open sea.

Soon after dark, *Endeavour* was becalmed and found herself being swept by the tide towards one of the outer islands, coming close enough for Tupaia to be able to talk to people ashore. The linesman reported 13 fathoms [78 feet; 23 metres] but the seabed was too foul to risk dropping the anchor and it getting stuck. Frantically, the sailors lowered the pinnace with great difficulty in the darkness, getting it caught on a gun, and burly oarsmen pulled the ship to safety. They were saved from catastrophe by a light southerly arriving at just the right moment.

Tokerau Bay wasn't quite finished with *Endeavour*. Around midnight, Cook and those not on watch were settling down to sleep when there was an almighty jolt as the ship's hull struck a submerged rock. During their stay, the officers had inspected the wide entrance to the bay for hidden dangers, but this one they had missed. Fortunately the ship came safely off with no damage. Cook's mention of this incident in his journal is typically brief; on the large-scale chart is written Whale Rock, the 'Rock on which we struck'.

Surviving two near-disasters in one night made Cook thankful to get out to sea in a fresh westerly. The next day he spent hours doing the difficult calculations required to establish his longitude position, while the master's mate, Richard Pickersgill, began plotting his own chart of this coast, which would eventually show the country's northern limits.

Tricky onshore winds slowed their progress past the Cavalle Isles and the deep bay Cook named Doubtless Bay. Ten or so canoes came to visit but kept their distance until Tupaia persuaded them to come close enough to trade cloth for 'goodly quantities' of fish.

He was also able to talk to the paddlers and relay to Cook and Banks the startling news that three days rowing [paddling] in their canoes, at a place called Muriwhenua, the land would take a short turn to the southward and from thence, recorded Banks, 'extend no more to the West'.

Endeavour was now close to the latitude of Cape Maria van Diemen on Tasman's chart. Were they about to approach this same cape *from the east*, and find themselves turning south and, with no land out to the west, running down the coast that the Dutchmen had sailed up nearly 140 years earlier?

Three days of frustrating light winds forced Cook to make five or six tacks along the bleak stretch of coast overlooked by a prominent hill. Cook named it Mount Camel — 'A Camel standing on a desert'. No country upon Earth, he thought, could look more barren than this bay. There were villages, canoes and white sand dunes to be seen near the shoreline, but Cook wondered if the complete lack of vegetation on the inland ridges indicated that the land 'lies open to the Western Sea'.

His intuition would prove correct, but on the morning of Wednesday 13 December, it began to blow.

Ask experienced mariners to name the stormiest, most dangerous seas on the planet? Usually, lists begin with the globe-circling Southern Ocean, especially south of Cape Horn through the notorious Drake Passage. Then comes the Bay of Biscay, west of France, and some parts of the Indian Ocean and the South China Sea prone to seasonal typhoons.

Also among the leaders are the seas around New Zealand's north and western coasts: first, the passage known as Cook Strait between the North and South Islands, then the turbulent seas found off Cape Reinga and North Cape, where the Pacific meets the Tasman. And further, the notorious 1000-mile expanse of the Tasman Sea itself, whose fierce westerlies blow onto the entire length of both islands.

Endeavour and the ninety-one men aboard her were about to be tested to the limits of their endurance by New Zealand's coastal weather systems.

Cook's chart reveals the nightmare that engulfed him for the next three weeks. In kinder weather he might have rounded North Cape and Cape Reinga a few miles offshore, keeping the coastline well in sight, before turning south.

Instead, the chart shows that after leaving Sandy Bay, *Endeavour* was driven by high adverse winds and huge swells more than 50 miles northeast, out of sight of land for the first time since Poverty Bay. A week of gales and she was over 100 miles away, northwest of the Cape, as far north to 33 degrees latitude and literally off the chart.

Working aloft, especially bringing in topgallant sails shredded by gale-force winds, required strength, agility and nerves of steel. Sailors stood on swaying footropes and leaned over the yards to untie, reef or change a sail. Only from mid-twentieth century were square-rigger crews required to use safety harnesses.

It's not hard to imagine how frustrating and lonely this must have felt. Cook knew of the Tonga archipelago some 1500 miles to the northeast. But he had no idea what lay west of New Zealand, other than the western coastline of New Holland [Australia] thousands of miles away. *Endeavour* was all but lost in a measureless ocean.

So when the winds allowed, Cook kept turning south, back to where he knew New Zealand's tip lay. On Christmas Day they sighted the Three Kings Islands, so-named by Tasman. Several gannets shot by Banks during a lull in the bad weather provided a festive dinner for a drunken crew.

It was only a temporary reprieve. Three days later the gale had increased to what Cook called a hurricane, with seas he described as 'prodigious high'. Four more days of hell passed before they sighted Cape Maria van Diemen again. On New Year's Day Cook realised that he was seeing Mount Camel from the *western* side of the peninsula. The ship was now battling such a gale of westerly wind he believed it would have proved fatal had he not kept well offshore. In the midst of summer and in the latitude of 35 degrees S. he wrote, 'such a Gale of wind … which for its Strength and Continuance' he had hardly ever experienced before.

Endeavour was lucky to survive this storm, which lasted nearly three weeks. Cook was not the only man on board who'd never seen weather and seas as terrifying in all their decades of sailing. His journal during this period tells of sailors repeatedly ordered aloft to reef the sails

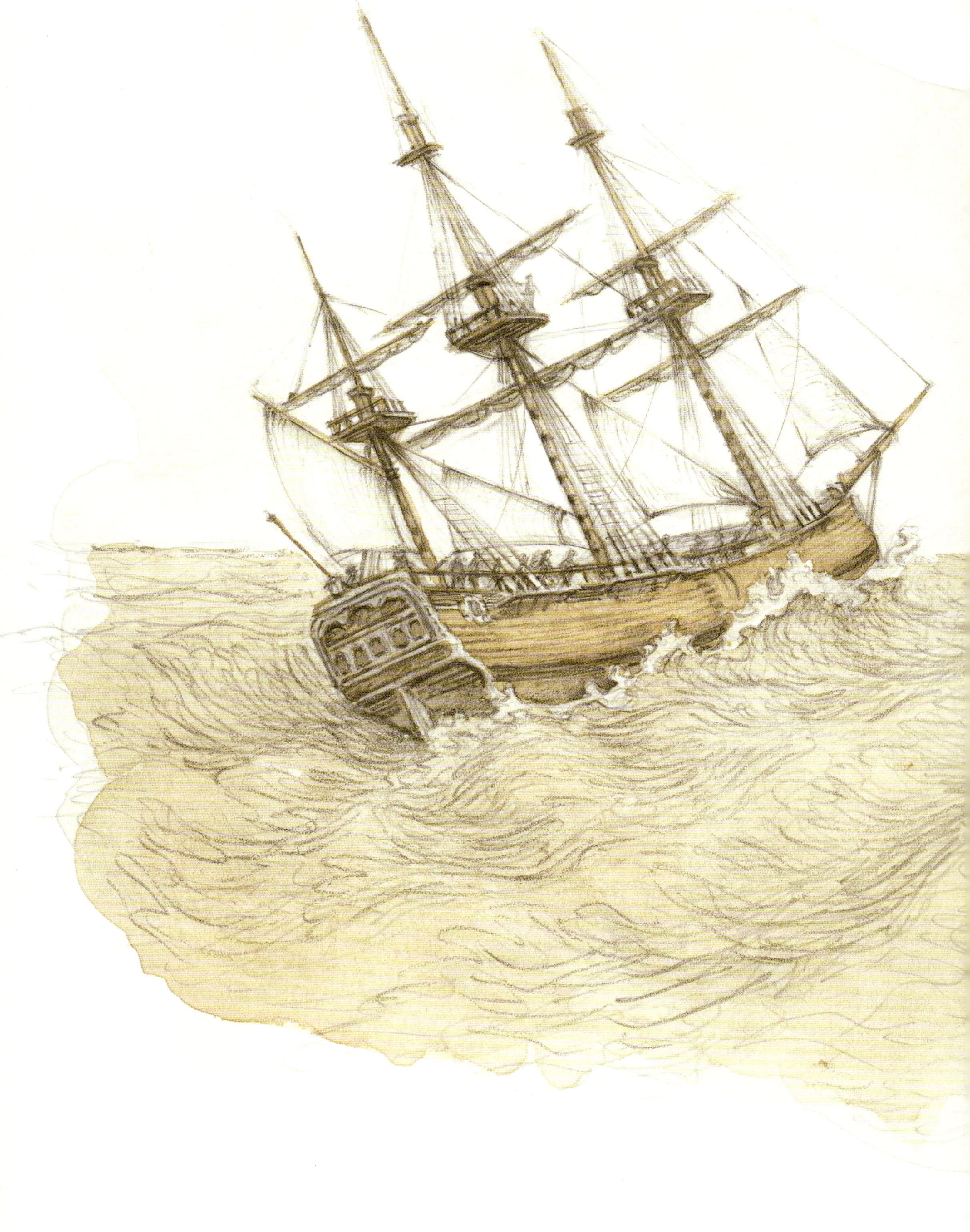

Off North Cape, *Endeavour* struck atrocious weather that lasted for nearly three weeks. Even under reduced sail, the ship was driven some fifty miles north-east of land, then over 100 miles out to the south-west. [After a sketch by Sydney Parkinson, 'The *Endeavour* in stormy seas', 1769.]

— a dangerous task even for fit and agile young men as the ship rolled and plunged deep into the troughs of mountainous swells. Great white-topped waves broke over the decks, drenching the two or three men needed on the helm. Sailors on deck handling ropes were at continual risk of being swept overboard. The sailmaker was kept busy below repairing torn canvas.

The journal also shows that for all these stormy weeks Cook was constantly taking sights, recording the latitude and the ship's exact course. Despite being out of sight of land for long periods in atrocious weather, he still saw enough to add the northern tip of New Zealand to the chart with pinpoint accuracy.

While the storm raged, Cook's superb ship-handling, constant attention to navigation and the utmost caution saved *Endeavour* from the very real possibilities of being caught over-canvassed, foundering in monstrous seas or being wrecked on a lee shore.

Or, the unlikely possibility of seeing another ship through the murk. If it had not been for the bad weather *Endeavour* and the much larger *St Jean Baptiste* [650 tons] may well have sighted each other. On 13 December the French explorer Jean François Marie de Surville had passed within fifty miles south of Cook on his way eastwards to rounding North Cape and anchor in Doubtless Bay, where *Endeavour* had been only a week earlier.

De Surville made two good charts while in New Zealand waters: the east-west coastline between Cape Maria van Diemen and North Cape, then Doubtless Bay itself. But his expedition ended unhappily: the same hurricane which hit *Endeavour* damaged the French ship anchored in Doubtless Bay. Repairs were begun, but troubles with local Māori forced him to put hurriedly to sea with most of his crew sick or dying from scurvy. Somehow he made it across the Pacific, only to drown trying to land in heavy seas on the coast of Peru to get help for his men.

As the New Year dawned and the winds finally began to abate, *Endeavour* was now running down 'The Desert Coast' that we know as Ninety Mile Beach. 'Nothing is to be seen but long sand Hills,' Cook wrote, 'with hardly any Green thing upon them.'

Nevertheless, after an uneasy few hours being set by adverse winds rather too close for comfort to the entrance of the Kaipara Harbour, Cook the resolute surveyor surprisingly turned his ship north again. Simply to better examine the coast on the return run, he took *Endeavour* back north to within sight of Mount Camel and Cape Maria van Diemen. It was, he concluded from a safer distance, a desolate, most inhospitable and dangerous coast, which he was determined not to come as close to again.

Between 7 and 16 January *Endeavour* continued south, with Cook keeping his distance from land but also searching for a harbour which he could confidently enter. The severe battering off the northern coast had taken its toll: the ship needed to be careened for scrubbing down and painting, repairs had to be done, sails mended. Water and wood must be found, sooner rather than later. No doubt the sailors were bone-weary and the scientists yearning to set foot on dry land. And there was little of interest to see, just a few albatrosses circling the ship, and, on shore, infrequent fires or houses indicating habitation.

There were indeed several large harbours on this long and desolate coast, but after his unpleasant recent experience off the Kaipara Harbour, Cook was taking no risks. The considerable harbours of Manukau, Raglan and Kawhia he passed by — just as well, as all are tidal, shallow and even today the marked channels through their tricky bars and sandbanks are treated by skippers with great caution.

The closest he got was to Raglan Harbour, passing a small island almost completely covered with birds. Banks thought they were gannets, thus its name, Gannet Island.

The next day a snow-clad mountain unexpectedly came into view to the south, something Tasman and Visscher had evidently not seen. Here was an isolated and magnificent peak 'of a prodigious height', even in summer topped with snow. Cook compared it to the 'Pike of Teneriffe' in the Canary Islands. 'Certainly it is the noblest hill I have ever seen,' enthused Banks. Cook named it Mount Egmont in tribute to one of his sponsors, John Perceval, the Earl of Egmont and a previous First Lord of the Admiralty. To the tribes of the area, it was known as Taranaki.

For the three days that it took *Endeavour* to round Cape Egmont, the snows were mostly obscured by cloud, but Cook was impressed with the surrounding fertile countryside. Two oddly shaped islands on the northern side of the cape became the Sugar-Loaf Isles. As Mount Egmont dropped astern, he knew *Endeavour* was steadily approaching the large bay marked on Tasman's chart, and where the Dutchman's two ships *Heemskerk* and *Zeehaen* had dropped anchor.

Cook was also well aware of Tasman's tragic first encounter with local Māori — four of his crew killed — and that he had quickly upped anchor to explore what he called Murderer's Bay [now Golden Bay]. Understandably cautious, Tasman had not risked a landing, and bad weather had prompted him to proceed north.

One question Tasman's chart had not answered. Were the lofty green hills Cook was now seeing all around him just the embracing arms of a very large bay? Or could this be a strait between two islands, with a navigable passage to the south that went through to 'the Eastern Sea'? Tasman and Visscher had studied the tidal flows and suspected that there was such a passage.

If so, Cook's chart headed Aeheinomouwe would almost certainly show that it was a large island, not any part of a Great Southern Continent. Cook the surveyor was determined to settle the matter.

CAPE STEPHENS

BLIND BAY

Stephens Isle
Admiralty Isles

CAPE FAREWELL

ADMIRALTY BAY
POINT JACKSON

Jocks Point

QUEEN CHARLOTTES SOUND

CAPE KOAMAROO

CAPE TARAWHITTE

CLOUDY BAY

CAPE CAMPBEL

SNOWEY MOUNTAINS

C O O K S

Lookers on

Var. 15. 4 E

GORES BAY

BANKS'S ISLAND

Var. 14. 30 E.

7

At Ship Cove

The morning of 15 January dawned with fickle light airs as *Endeavour* approached the first of many deep bays and inlets of the sounds known to Māori as Totara-nui. It was an undignified entrance, with the tide requiring oarsmen in the small boats to pull the *Endeavour* clear of a reef on one side and some rocky islands on the other. Watching this ungainly exercise were the inhabitants of a nearby pā and a distant canoe, along with a curious 'Sea Lyon' which twice rose near the ship to sniff the air.

By early afternoon, the boats had towed *Endeavour* the length of the larger island of Motuara. Ahead lay a beautiful little cove with two beaches of white sand, backed by steep bush-clad hills. After seven weeks at sea, at least four battling onshore gales, this 'very Snug Cove' must have seemed to Cook and his crew as much like paradise as Matavai Bay had been on arriving in Tahiti.

It was a perfect anchorage, good holding in 11 fathoms. Abundant varieties of fish and seafood were there for the taking. The rich birdlife included shags, tui, oystercatchers, wood pigeon and bellbirds, whose dawn song Banks thought was 'the most melodious wild musick' he ever heard. Ashore was a stream of excellent fresh water and the wood of 'one intire forest'. Named by Cook as Ship Cove, Meretoto became his favourite Pacific anchorage, which he revisited on his two later voyages.

Respectful relationships were quickly established with local Māori. Soon after anchoring, four canoes carrying about sixty-five warriors visited the ship. After their ritual displays of defiance, an important elder named Topaa was welcomed on board by Tupaia, followed by others.

Cook was sufficiently confident to order the ship to be careened, and the scrubbing of the starboard side of the hull began immediately. The three weeks that *Endeavour* lay in Ship Cove were put to productive toil. The ship was righted after only three days, her hull newly painted and caulked. The coopers repaired the water casks, others worked on the rigging, fixed the tiller mechanism and other ironwork. Fishing on a daily basis with both nets and lines seldom failed to get fish 'sufficient for all hands'. Gangs went ashore to collect wood, water, and vegetables and to cut grass for the ship's sheep. They collected stones as ballast, to add weight

The kōkako was among the native birds whose song entranced Joseph Banks at Ship Cove. The tree-clad hill probably featured the bright scarlet summer-flowering southern rata. Earlier, as *Endeavour* sailed during November around East Cape and the Coromandel Peninsula, Banks had noted the coastal pōhutukawa, 'an excellent timber tree … which bears a very conspicuous scarlet flower made up [of] many threads, and is a large tree as big as an oak in England, has a very heavy hard wood …'

to *Endeavour's* stern. The first Sunday, the men were given leave to go to the watering place ashore and enjoy the calm sunny weather 'as they thought proper'.

For Cook, Tupaia, Banks and the scientists, their wide-ranging explorations of Totara-nui during these three busy weeks were to produce some surprising discoveries, both pleasant and otherwise.

Ever since landing at Poverty Bay, now three months earlier, the question of cannibalism had remained unanswered and probably little discussed. To superstitious seamen the very thought was horrifying; no less so to the young, better-educated officers. Tupaia had made his disgust clear to Cook and Banks when the subject was first mentioned during the encounters in Poverty Bay. Cook's later writings indicate that he felt the practice could be more tolerantly regarded as 'customary' and would diminish with the coming of 'more humane times'.

But on only their second day in the sounds, Cook and party were confronted by direct evidence: on a beach not far from Ship Cove, they found a small group of Māori with human remains that had clearly been recently cooked and eaten. Cook records that 'finding this bone with part of the sinews fresh upon it was stronger proof than any we had yet met with'. To be fully persuaded, they suggested that it could be a bone from a dog, but the Māori 'with great fervency, took hold of his Fore Arm, and told us again that it was that bone: and to convince us that they had eat the flesh he took hold of the flesh of his own Arm with his teeth and made Signs of Eating'. Two days later, exploring inland, some sailors found further proof: three hip bones beside an umu [native oven of heated stones set into the ground].

It was little comfort to the Europeans to be reassured by Tupaia, following discussions with the locals, that only the bodies of enemies slain in conflict were eaten. This explained why a woman's corpse spied the previous day floating in the water had not been eaten; it had been weighted with stones by her relatives, the usual local burial custom, but had risen to the surface.

Nor were the sailors pleased to watch Banks trading the severed head of a young male, one of four dried heads brought out to the ship, for a pair of white linen drawers. The boy had apparently died from a blow to the temple. The other skulls the old man Topaa would not trade at any price, not even to the wilful and persistent Banks. His journal coolly supposes the skulls were kept as trophies, 'as possibly scalps were by the North Americans before the Europeans came among them; the brains were however, taken out as we had been told, maybe they are a delicacy here. The flesh and skin upon these heads were soft but they were somehow preservd so as not to stink at all'. It's the first European mention of the practice; fifty years later, between about 1820 and 1840, European collectors were paying high prices for dried Māori heads, preferably tattooed.

However disturbing this new knowledge was, it did not deter Cook from his own goals: to explore and chart the sounds [which he named for Queen Charlotte, wife of George III] and to determine if there was a passage through to the eastern sea. From 18 January, the ship now safely righted, he set out daily with the scientists in the pinnace to survey the Sounds' many inlets, islands and coves.

Tupaia accompanied them everywhere, 'of infinite service' in the encounters with local people. The Māori of this area, Cook later wrote, appeared to be only about 300 or 400 in number, darker in skin and poor compared to those in the north. Their canoes were without ornament and, lacking flat ground on which to establish gardens, they lived mainly on fish, seafoods and fern roots. He noted that only a few seemed to be tattooed.

On 23 January, Cook's patient exploring gave him the answer he sought. Setting off with Banks and Solander to row to the head of the inlet, some twenty miles distant, he decided instead to land on the southeastern side of the sound and climb a prominent peak.

Since boyhood, Cook had climbed hills, but few climbs had been as rewarding as on this day. Leaving the scientists to their botanising, and taking one sailor with him, he reached the top of Kaiteapeha, on Arapawa Island. The views in every direction were spectacular but more than that, 'I was abundantly recompensed for the trouble I had in ascending the Hill,' he wrote, 'for from it I saw what I took to be the Eastern Sea, and a Strait or passage from it into the Western Sea.'

From the top of Kaiteapeha on Arapawa Island, Cook saw the distant open waters that confirmed local Māori knowledge of a passage existing between the 'Eastern sea' and the 'Western sea'. On Joseph Banks' urging, he wrote 'Cook's Straights' on the chart.

The implications of this for European knowledge of the whole Pacific, and theories of a Great Southern Continent, were immense.

His journal gives no hint of the jubilation he must have felt, but Banks noted that on his return from the climb, Cook seemed to be in high spirits, 'having seen the Eastern sea and satisfied himself of the existence of a streight communicating with it …'

Typically, in the next week he climbed two more high vantage points to further convince himself of 'the Greatest probability in the World' that a passage existed. On both hilltops he left cairns of stones, with silver coins, musket balls and beads, oddments that would stand the test of time, a witness to British visits.

After the third climb, Cook was understandably keen to put to sea. The survey of the whole of Totara-nui was sufficiently complete, with only minor sections near the head of the inlet remaining on the map as dotted lines.

On the last day of the month the ship's carpenter presented Cook with two stout posts, inscribed with the ship's name, month and year. One was erected with the Union flag at the watering place near the ship's anchorage. For approval to erect the other on Motuara Island, Cook took Tupaia to visit the island's pā. This post, Tupaia explained, would be to any other European ship proof of *Endeavour*'s visit. Cook records that with chief Topaa's 'free consent',

75

One of Cook's closest calls on his circumnavigation of New Zealand came shortly after leaving the Sounds. Gripped by strong tides, unable to make steerage way in the light airs, even with her anchor dropped as a desperate last measure, *Endeavour* drifted helplessly towards the rocky Two Brothers islands.

and moreover, a further promise never to pull it down, the post with its Union flag was then hoisted. Cook named the inlet Queen Charlotte's Sound and 'took formal possession of it and adjacent lands in the Name of and for the Use of His Majesty'. With a bottle of wine, a toast was drunk and the empty bottle presented to Topaa, 'with which he was highly pleased'.

The next day, 1 February, preparations for sea intensified. Men were sent ashore to cut and make brooms. The last collections of wood and 'sellery' were loaded, fresh water too, although ten small casks ready at the watering place to be taken aboard were washed out into the cove by the heavy rain flooding the stream, never to be found.

A significant conversation took place in these last days, now Cook's longest stay in any New Zealand anchorage. On their visit to Topaa's island pā, Cook and Tupaia had acquired some local knowledge of a strait and beyond it two or maybe three lands. These were Tovypoenammu, a land to the southwest and named for the prized greenstone found there, used for tools and ornaments, and Cook's oddly spelled Aeheinomouwe [probably an attempt at Te Ika o Maui/North Island] that would take 'a great many Moons' to sail around.

Cook had sailed nearly around the one. Now the other, the greenstone land with that tantalising fragment of a western coastline charted by Tasman and Visscher, awaited.

Before *Endeavour* hoisted sail and slowly took her leave of Meretoto cove, Topaa came on board to say farewell. His final words reaffirmed for Cook and Tupaia the existence of a passage into the Eastern sea and, according to Banks' account, 'that the Land to the South consisted of 2 Islands or several which might be saild round in 3 or 4 days in their canoes; that he knew of no other great land than that we had been upon.'

Topaa's farewell may have been informative and affable, and Banks sad to be leaving without getting to know the people better, but after his final visit to the pā, Cook wrote that some seemed not sorry for their departure. Indeed, though they had sold their fish freely enough, some showed 'clear signs of disapprobation.'

On 7 February, in a light northwesterly, *Endeavour* finally cleared the entrance to Totaranui, and turned south into the promised strait. Here, just on sunset and throughout a terrifying night, *Endeavour*'s epic Pacific voyage very nearly came to an abrupt end.

For most of their three weeks at anchor, *Endeavour*'s men had gone about their work in summer sunshine. There'd been a few days of heavy rain, and on 2 February a full storm hit, with winds off the land strong enough to break one of the ship's hawsers tied to a tree ashore. But while passing through 'Cook's Straights', *Endeavour* did not have to face any of the high seas and strong winds for which the area was later to become famous.

Atrocious conditions are not, however, the strait's only hazards. Nursing *Endeavour* in light airs around Cape Koamaru, the most eastern tip of Arapawa Island, Cook is confronted by a group of small craggy islands that he oddly names The Two Brothers. Though about four miles distant, he anticipates they can be comfortably cleared to starboard. But as the light fades the wind also dies away. *Endeavour* is soon being carried by a strong ebb tide, close to these islands and into extreme peril.

Basic seamanship and a good measure of luck save the ship. Hearing the linesman call 75 fathoms, Cook immediately orders the anchor dropped, and 150 fathoms of cable are rapidly let out. Even this manoeuvre is no match for the tide, running at about five knots. The noise of breakers and swirling whirlpools at the base of the nearer island grow horribly louder by the minute.

Endeavour carried two weighty cast-iron anchors, not only for intentional anchoring but also for emergency use in arresting a sailing ship's drift towards a hazard.

Every man on board is by now certain this sunset will be their last. The ship will be pinned against the rocks, to be broken up by the surging waves of the next big storm. In a matter of months, even weeks, there will be no trace of either the vessel or her crew.

At midnight, the tide and their luck change. As *Endeavour* is carried by a whisker past the nearest outcrop of rock, the sailors begin to heave in the anchor on its enormous length of rope hawser. In the dark, the job takes three hours. Mercifully, just before dawn, a light northerly springs up, enabling Cook to set a safe course to the southernmost land in sight.

That night was a dramatic prelude to *Endeavour*'s run the next day, down the passage to become known as Cook Strait. He placed the name on his chart but never refers to it in his journals — only with some persuasion from Banks had he agreed that for this important passage, 'Cook' was the appropriate name.

Running confidently before fresh northerlies, *Endeavour* now had substantial land on both sides: to port, the southern extremities of the northern island, and to starboard the snow-topped Kaikoura range of a landmass still uncharted.

He could have simply proceeded south. However, a conversation among the officers over dinner prompted him to a change of plan, to prove to everyone beyond doubt that Aeheinomouwe was in fact an island — that there was no isthmus or other connection to a southern continent that some still believed to exist

From what he'd learned from the inhabitants of Totara-nui and his own observations, Cook was very nearly convinced that there was no landmass anywhere to the southeast. But admittedly, his chart of the northern island was still incomplete, so he turned *Endeavour* east, passing Cape Palliser [named after his former captain and good friend]. Three large and ornamented canoes put out from the Cape Palliser shore, their paddlers' friendliness and eagerness to trade nails indicating that they knew of the visitors. Off Castle Point [now Castlepoint] two more canoes came alongside, trading their catches of fish.

The diversion to the north, about twenty miles, was quickly accomplished. On 9 February the weather cleared to allow a view of Cape Turnagain, about seven leagues distant [twenty-one nautical miles] but close enough to recognise the land's characteristic features. Cook called his officers on deck.

'I asked them if they were now satisfied that this land was an Island; to which they answer'd in the Affirmative.' Cook promptly turned *Endeavour* to the east and the next day, to the south.

With latitudes once more being recorded by Cook's regular sightings, Cape Turnagain, Castle Point and Cape Palliser dropped astern. The outline of Aeheinomouwe was finally complete.

OPEN BAY
CASCADES POINT
MISTAKEN BAY

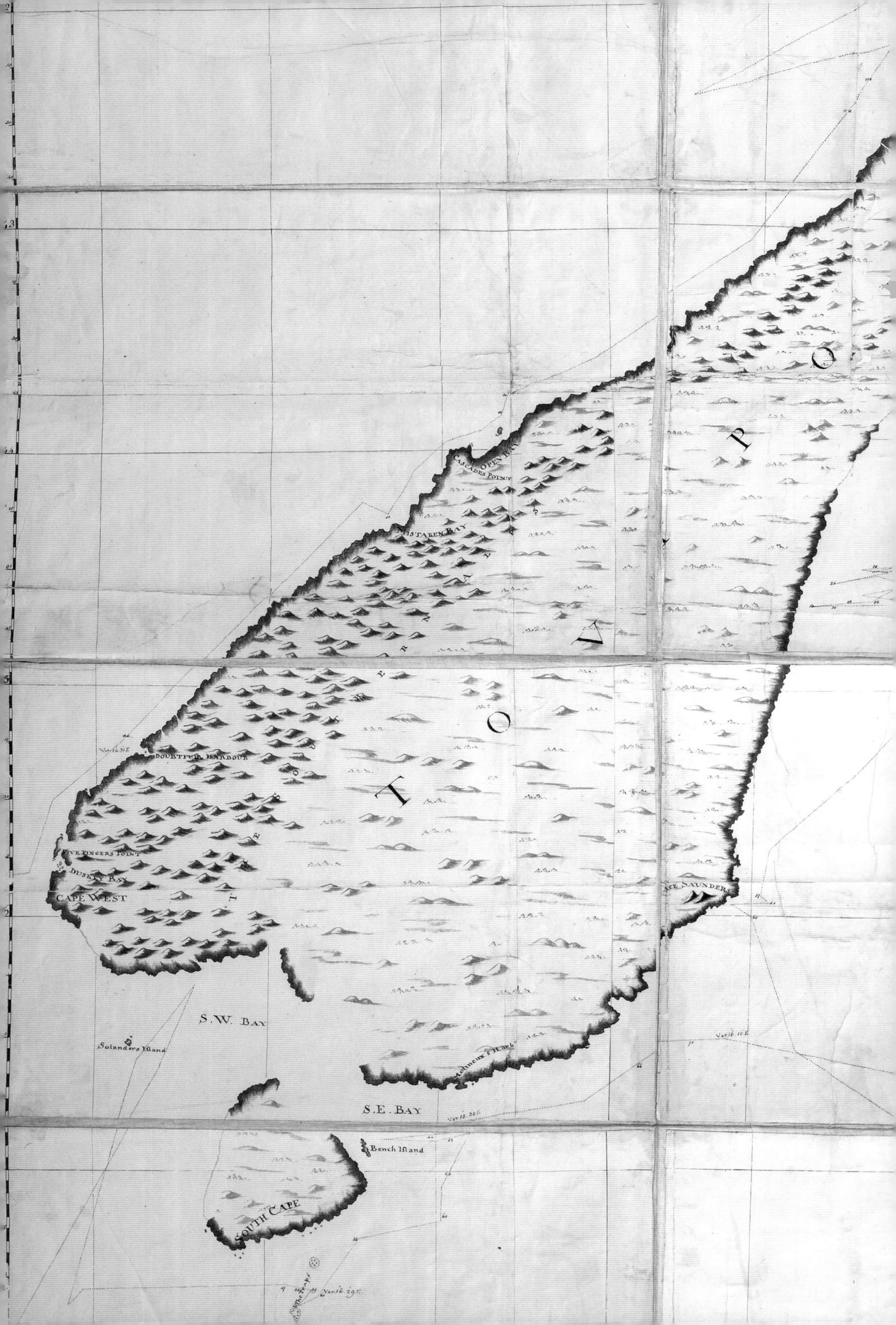

DOUBTFUL HARBOUR

FIVE FINGERS POINT
DUSKY BAY
CAPE WEST

CAPE SAUNDERS

S.W. BAY
Solander's Island
Molineux's Isles
S.E. BAY

Bench Island
SOUTH CAPE

8

Deep South

Endeavour had now been on the New Zealand coast for four months. Since arriving at Poverty Bay, all on board had learned a good deal about the Māori inhabitants, their dress, culture and language, gardening and seagoing traditions. Many of the officers had kept journals that later told the world about this newest addition to European knowledge of the Pacific. The naturalists would display thousands of specimens of exotic new plants, trees and marine life, and the artists' many sketches of landscapes, canoes, villages, fortified pā and portraits of the inhabitants would be widely published.

They had survived a hurricane, many gales, more than a few narrow escapes from shipwreck and some tricky encounters with Māori — any one of which could easily have ended in disaster.

From 12 February and for the next six weeks, the greenstone land was to provide a very different experience. As summer weather gave way to autumnal squalls, the challenges would be entirely nautical.

Little evidence was seen of any Māori habitation: only rarely smoke from inland fires, and just one canoe visit at the start of the circumnavigation.

Some 15 to 20 miles off the Kaikoura coast, *Endeavour* was ghosting along in conditions calm enough for Banks to shoot seabirds from a small boat. The surprising approach, so far out from the shore, of four double canoes carrying 57 men had Banks and his crew scrambling back aboard the ship, but despite Tupaia's overtures of friendliness, the canoes kept their distance. Banks thought they seemed more astonished than anything else. Perhaps word of this very strange vessel had not yet reached so far south?

As the sun dropped below the Kaikoura range, *Endeavour*'s men watched the four canoes paddle back towards the land. This was the farthest out any canoes had ventured during their whole four months on the coast. As they vanished into the dusk, it was clear they would be paddling half of the way home in the dark. These were the last people *Endeavour* would encounter.

From the steep Kaikoura coastline until well south of Stewart Island, the course charted by Cook on Folio 16 now displays some puzzling zig-zags well away from land.

In late February 'a proper Storm' with enormous swells forced *Endeavour* far away from the coast, by 2 March to about 150 miles south-east of Cape Saunders [near today's Dunedin] and to a latitude of 48 degrees, actually south of Stewart Island.

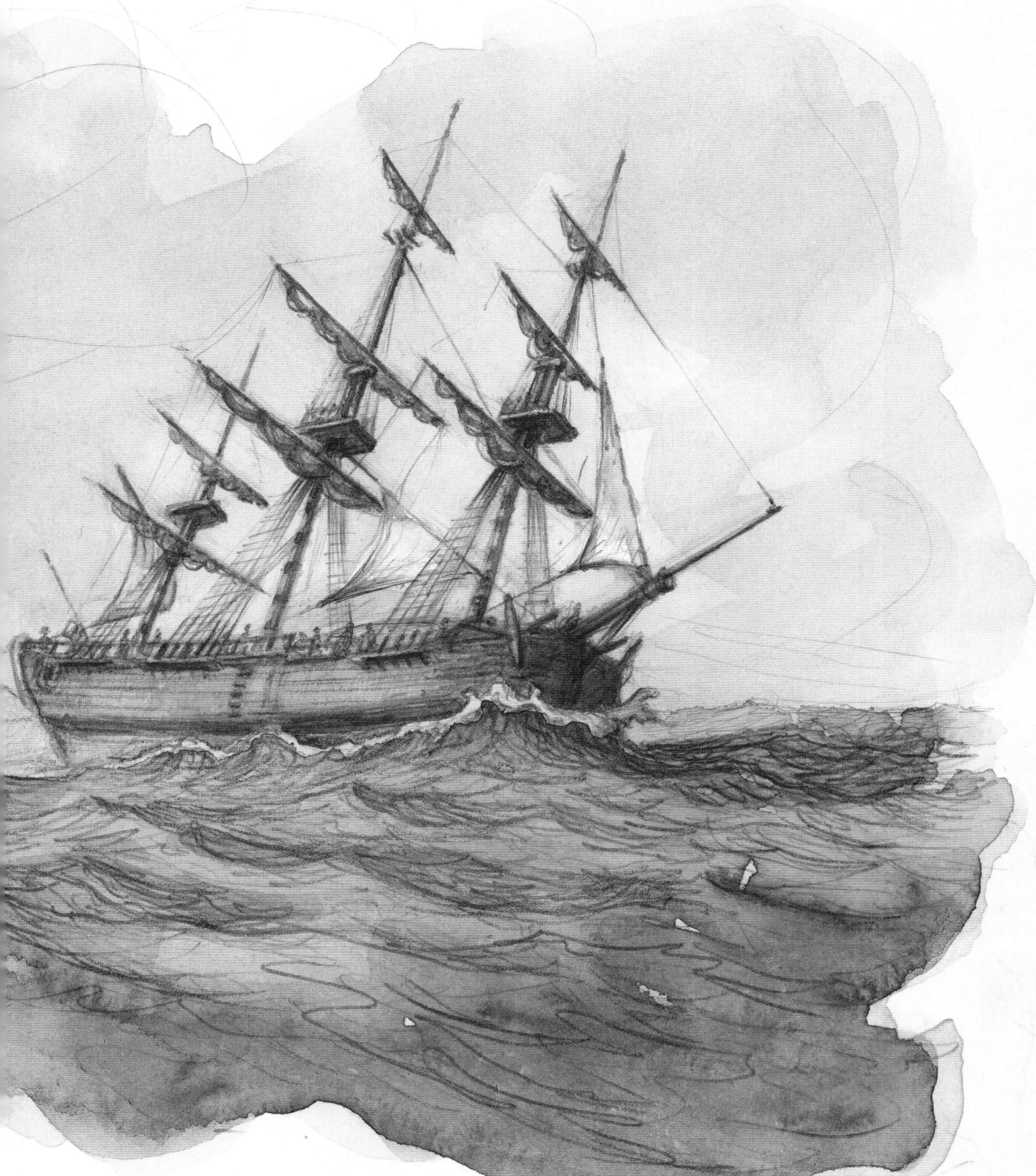

On 17 February *Endeavour* sailed past an important geographical feature, which Cook was confident was an island. He called it Banks's Island, much pleasing his fellow traveller. The ship passed close enough to the southeastern tip to see fires and some people. Why, that afternoon, did Cook not complete the survey of the southern side of Banks's Island, confirming it to be a peninsula? Why, instead, did he order the helmsmen to steer *Endeavour* southeast, away from the coast?

The reason was the continuing debate on board between the 'Continents', led by Banks and Gore, and the 'No Continents,' led rather more discreetly by Cook. On the morning watch, Gore announced he had spotted land to the southeast. Despite his own view that it was merely cloud, Cook ordered the change of course. He did not wish anyone to accuse him of leaving land unexplored.

Some seventy miles later, most on board generally agreed that that 'Mr Gore's imaginary land' was just that, an illusion. A disconsolate Banks writes that night that his 'Continents' party is now so small that there are 'no more heartily of it than myself and one poor midshipman, the rest begin to sigh for roast beef'.

So Cook, no doubt feeling quietly vindicated, turned back towards the land, expecting, from what he'd heard from chief Topaa as he departed from Totara-nui, that soon he would be rounding the southernmost point of the greenstone island.

A major surprise awaited him. *Endeavour* was gradually closing in on a substantial coastline that stretched far away to both north and south. Frustratingly, fresh southerlies kept her tacking back and forth [off today's Timaru] for the next five days, unable to make headway south. But when the weather cleared on 23 February they saw that the land ahead was 'high and Mountainous.' Cook was beginning to think that this country was rather more extensive than the chief Topaa had led him to believe. A four-day circumnavigation hardly seemed possible.

A straightforward run down the coast to find the southern extremity was not to be. Cook rarely erred in his judgement of how much sail to carry, but on 25 February he was keen to make the most of a fresh northerly gale. Over-canvassed, the ship lost the highest section of her mainmast, the main topgallant mast, and also a fore topmast studding sail boom. Both were replaced, but only after hours of frantic activity to control the sails, then lower and extricate the broken wooden topmast from the complex rigging. Only then could the new topmast could be raised and secured.

After this exhausting incident, and uncertain of the coastline's direction, Cook 'brought to' for the night about five miles off land. At first light, he made sail again, intending to press on south. He was conscious of his unfinished chart, the unanswered questions. The bitterly cold winds and chilly temperatures below decks were reminders of the coming autumn. Those essential supplies of wood, water and green vegetables on board wouldn't last for ever.

His decision not to seek shelter in one of several bays seen near Cape Saunders [named for a commander from his Quebec days] cost Cook dearly. The next day the wind further freshened, 'whistling all around the compass, sometimes blowing a fresh Gale, and at other times almost Calm'. *Endeavour* was driven away towards the southeast, well out of sight of land.

The sailors were constantly reefing or shaking out sails, or replacing several split 'all to pieces' by vicious gusts. At least once the high topgallant yards or even the topgallant masts were brought down on deck to reduce windage. In the conditions, handling sails was bad enough but lowering a yard or topmast was a difficult and extremely dangerous undertaking; once an able seaman himself, Cook would not have asked it of his sailors without good cause.

The gale increased in fury until it was 'a proper Storm', with drenching rain, vicious squalls and huge seas persisting without respite for more than twenty-four hours. Cook's journal records little more than the sail handling, wind direction and of course, the daily discipline of sightings and time-consuming mathematical calculations, regardless of the weather or the ship's rolling and pitching.

On 2 March, Cook recorded that *Endeavour* had reached the latitude of 48 degrees. The ship was about 150 miles from land, and although the weather had abated, the continuing huge swells from the southwest made him ever more certain there was no landmass in that direction.

It was time to get back to the coast, to establish once and for all whether he was sailing around a large island. But it wasn't until two days later that favourable winds allowed him to stand to the west 'with all the sail we could make' and, sighting Cape Saunders [near Dunedin] again, realise how much time and energy had been lost to the worst weather of the southern Pacific.

The sight of whales and seals playing in the boisterous, white-capped seas, along with a couple of small penguins that swam as fast as the ship while 'shrieking like a goose', must have provided the sailors with some entertainment, if only briefly. With any luck, the latitude of 48 degrees was as far south as their captain was going to take them.

By 5 March, back at latitude 46 degrees, Cook was heading resolutely west, keeping the coast running to the south of Cape Saunders well in his sights. For two days they saw smoke from a very large inland fire. It was the only sign of habitation, leading Banks to suppose the people to be 'very thinly scattered over this very large country'. He was correct. Compared with the North Island, there were few pā around Tovypoenammu's coasts. Even fewer Māori had penetrated inland to the river valleys in the west and south, where the precious greenstone was found.

Three days sailing in fickle weather made observations and charting unusually tricky. And unknown to Cook, the strong tides of the area resulted in some unusual miscalculations of the ship's course. His journal entries for 8 to 11 March speculate that the land he has approached from the east, and then observed from the south and west, is an island of some substance, but he does not draw it on the chart as an island or tentatively as a peninsula. Instead, lacking his usual certainty, he leaves the north-eastern coast of Stewart Island and the facing portion of the mainland coast conspicuously blank. [It would be the sealing ship *Pegasus* that in 1809 named the island after the first mate, William Stewart.]

And in his summary presented to the Admiralty, notable for its confidence in his chart's accuracy, Cook is at pains to explain this rare uncertainty as he took *Endeavour* around the southernmost headlands of Stewart Island: '…The Coast as is laid down from Cape Saunders to Cape South is no doubt in many places very erroneous as we hardly ever were able to keep near the shore and were some times blowen off altogether.'

Yet even good weather could present hazards. During the night of Friday 9 March, *Endeavour* again came close to disaster. After a calm night, sunrise revealed that the ship was less than a mile to leeward of a reef 'on which the Sea broke very high'. Cook had barely enough room to tack the ship away from these rocks, and realised to his undoubted horror that there

Whales, porpoises, seals and penguins were frequently sighted from *Endeavour*'s decks. Joseph Banks recorded several whales seen six days before Nicholas Young sighted land, with greater numbers noted by Cook off Cape Saunders [near Dunedin] and as the ship rounded Stewart Island.

were more than a few others in the immediate area. With no warnings from the lookouts, the ship had sailed among these in the moonless night.

'It is apparent that we had a very fortunate Escape,' wrote Cook with masterly understatement. He named these reefs The Traps because they lie in wait to catch unwary strangers. [Today they are marked on Stewart Island charts as North Trap and South Trap.]

Celebrations were held that day, and not just to rejoice in their good fortune or the birthday of one of the officers. [They dined on roast dog, one of a litter born on board.] *Endeavour* had just sailed around the southernmost point of New Zealand; Latitude accurate at 47 degrees 19' south, Longitude with an error of only a few miles, 192 degrees 12' west from Greenwich.

At last, the majority 'No Continents' declared themselves triumphant. The land to starboard was described by Banks as steep conical hills topped with snow, presenting a most romantic appearance. As *Endeavour* rounded the point, Cook named it South Cape, to the total demolition, wrote Banks, 'of our aerial fabrick calld continent'. His spirits were not much revived by the impressive spectacle of large numbers of albatrosses circling the ship.

If the whole ship's crew hoped fervently for a straight northward run up the west coast of Tovypoenammu, they were to be disappointed. Cook straightaway turned north, but found himself closing on land which he decided [correctly] must be part of the mainland.

Another swift change of course and *Endeavour* was heading back southwest, passing small islands he named Solander's Isles. Frustratingly, fresh gales forced her even further back south, again almost to 48 degrees, before Cook was finally able, on 13 March, to turn the ship to the north.

The chart shows that between 13 and 25 March, favourable winds allowed Cook to follow the coastline northwards, keeping just as close as he dared to this long and dangerous lee shore. 'The face of the Country bears a very rugged Aspect,' he writes, 'being full of high craggy hills, on the Summits of which were several patches of Snow.' They could see wood on the hills and valleys, but no sign of inhabitants. Nowhere was he tempted to seek shelter, even when faced with a furious Joseph Banks determined to explore a promising harbour. On 14 March, beginning his run north from the very south-western tip of Tovypoenammu, Cook spied a narrow opening in the land, probably indicating a very snug harbour. The hills on each side rose almost perpendicular from the sea.

Cook reasoned that the winds would either blow right *into* the harbour most of the time, or right *out* maybe one day in a month. It would be 'highly imprudent' to risk his ship by trying to enter the harbour, and perhaps becoming trapped by the prevailing winds for what could be weeks.

Cook took *Endeavour* as close as he dared up the long western coastline of the South Island, ever mindful of the Tasman's dangerous onshore winds. He and Banks both wrote of the heavy surf, the thin strip of dense coastal forest and the craggy summits of the alpine range behind, snowcapped even in late summer.

With nightfall approaching and a fresh gale blowing, he decided to continue on, calling the inlet 'Duskey Bay' and also bypassing 'Doubtfull Harbour', for the same reason of safety.

Probably Banks was still smarting from the demolition of his pet 'southern continent' theory, but the decision to sail on past Duskey Sound rankled with him, not just at the time, but for many years. He and Solander had been cooped up on the ship for a whole month, since leaving Queen Charlotte's Sound. Naturally he wished to enter this promising inlet and go ashore, not only to botanise, but also to investigate the mineral outcrops spied from the ship along this part of the coast.

Cook stood firm, as any responsible master of a square-rigged ship would do when faced with strong and unreliable winds blowing onto a lee shore. Even after eighteen months on *Endeavour*, Banks evidently hadn't yet learned that safety of ship and crew outweighed all else.

[In March 1773, on his second Pacific voyage, Cook took *Resolution* into 'Duskey Bay' and spent six weeks there, exploring and charting the fjord.]

As *Endeavour* proceeds steadily north, Cook's journal tells us what was visible from several miles out to sea. Only a fresh gale on 20 March pushes him away to the southwest, from a cape he called Foulwind. Sighting four waterfalls streaming down impressive red cliffs, Cook names this feature Cascades Point. Further north, the narrow coastal strip is either thickly forested or as barren and rugged 'as any country upon earth'. Rising high above the flat strip, snow-covered alpine summits are glimpsed occasionally through cloud. [He does not see the highest peak, which is given his own name nearly eighty years later by Captain J.L. Stokes of the survey ship H.M.S. *Acheron*. Today it is also known by its Māori name, Aoraki.]

Like Abel Tasman before him, he is wary of the huge swells rolling onto long desolate stretches of beach. He notes that the snowy alpine range begins to lie further inland, and guesses, correctly, that there is a continued chain of high mountains from one end of the island to the other. He doesn't write Southern Alps on his chart, but is impressed by their grandeur: 'No country upon Earth can appear with a more rugged and barren Aspect than this doth; from the Sea for as far inland as the Eye can reach nothing is to be seen but the Summits of these rocky Mountains, which seem to lay so near one another as not to admit any Vallies between them ... it is very probable that great part of the land is taken up in Lakes, Ponds, etc ...'

And on 22 March he is yet again reminded of the perils of a lee shore in light airs: *Endeavour* is three or four miles from land, in 54 fathoms, when the wind drops away. The large swells, always from the southwest, now begin to carry the ship towards the beach where a huge surf is pounding. Cook is sufficiently apprehensive to consider dropping the anchor, but a light south-westerly arrives in time.

Triumphantly, on 24 March *Endeavour* rounds the northwesternmost point of Tovypoenammu, which Cook names Cape Farewell. Three days later his journal records without fuss that the circumnavigation of the whole country was now completed. 'It is time for me to think of quitting it.'

Looking for an anchorage after rounding Cape Farewell, *Endeavour* made little progress against light easterlies and in thick misty conditions. Ever cautious, Cook had the linesmen calling the depths day and night.

With the wind changing to the north and *Endeavour* picking up speed, Cook could now recognise Stephens Island and know that he had completed his circumnavigation of Tovypoenammu. But Ship Cove was still another twenty miles to the east, two or three days away, so he chose Admiralty Bay, where Tasman had anchored.

Endeavour sailed past Cape Farewell and into the unknown Tasman Sea on 1 April, 1770, with numerous completed charts of both New Zealand's main and offshore islands, sections of coastline and notable harbours. Working on the charts occupied Cook and his young assistants much of each day and into the evenings; the final charts were prepared from field sheets and preliminary compilations showing observations and positions recorded over a 24-hour period.

Despite high winds and rain, parties were soon ashore to gather wood and fill the many empty casks with fresh water. There were fish to be caught — Tupaia and Taiata caught almost a boat load, while sailors let down lines out of the cabin windows and as they had in Bream Bay earlier, in a single day hauled up nearly a hundred fish.

Otherwise, the bay offered little to weary mariners who had been seven continuous weeks at sea. Banks and Solander fought their way up hills through head-high fern to find only three new plants to add to the 400 already in their collection. No inhabitants were sighted, only some deserted huts. Cook went off exploring in the pinnace, noting other good anchorages offered by the sounds' many inlets and islands.

On 31 March, *Endeavour* is loaded with wood, water and 'sellery', and readied for sea. As the botanists' specimens have taken over the Great Cabin, Cook probably stores his newly completed 'Chart of New Zeland' safely in his cabin. There are also separate charts of the two major islands; he is particularly proud of the northern island's completeness and accuracy. He imagines the stir these charts will cause back in England. His young officers will make fair copies, to be forwarded if possible from a foreign port.

Characteristically, in the letter to Philip Stephens that he dispatches with copies of the charts and the journal from the first port-of-call, Batavia, Cook shares out the honours: 'Thus far I am certain that the Latitude and Longitude of few parts of the World are better settled than these. In this I was very much assisted by Mr Green [officially the astronomer] who let slip no one opportunity for making of Observations for setting the Longitude during the whole Course of the Voyage; and the many Valuable discoveries made by Mr Banks and Dr Solander in Natural History, and other things useful to the learned world, cannot fail of contributing very much to the Success of the Voyage.'

His officers and crew are not forgotten: '... I must say they have gone through the fatigues and dangers of the whole Voyage with that cheerfulness and Allertness that will always do Honour to British seamen ...' But from New Zealand, where to, next? Cook's journal tells us that he called his officers together and three options were discussed.

One was to proceed eastwards to Cape Horn through the southern ocean and on up the Atlantic to England. The second was to travel westwards through the southern Indian Ocean to enter the Atlantic by way of the Cape of Good Hope. The Admiralty instructions said only to choose 'the most Eligible way'.

Cook's own preference would have been by Cape Horn, offering a second chance to finally prove the existence *or not* of a *Terra Australis Incognita* lying south of Tahiti. But with the southern winter fast approaching, they all knew that *Endeavour* was in poor condition to risk the high latitudes of the Roaring Forties by way of either Cape.

The third option was to proceed due west, to fall in either with Visscher's coastline of a land he'd called Van Diemen's Land, or with the still unknown eastern coast of New Holland, wherever that was. Then, to follow this coast as far north as it went, and proceed to the East Indies or the island of Espiritu Santu, later to be identified in the archipelago that Cook named New Hebrides and now known as Vanuatu.

The voyage back to England would then be through seas already known to mariners.

Cook and his officers knew only too well that each of the three 12,000-mile passages back to England would present its own particular horrors for the ship and her crew.

They settled on the third option, to head west. But this decision, while the most sensible, proved fateful. Ahead lay further narrow escapes from shipwreck on reefs or lee shores, one nearly disastrous. Tragically, for a crew that was at this point unusually fit and healthy, thanks to Cook's insistence on fresh foods and general shipboard hygiene, there would soon be terrible loss of life, even before rounding the Cape of Good Hope.

At daylight on 1 April 1770, *Endeavour* raised sail and leaving Cape Farewell was set on a course westwards. Cook's journal at this point contains long passages on the still thorny question of the Great Southern Continent, which he has to admit might still exist. His voyage, he wrote, has shown that there is left 'but a small space to the Northward of 40 degrees where the grand object can lay ... I think it would be a great pity that this thing, which at times has been the Object of many Ages and Nations, should not now be wholy clear'd up; which might Easily be done in one Voyage, without either much trouble or danger or fear of Miscarrying, as the Navigator would know where to go to look for it; but if, after all, no Continent was to be found, then he might turn his thoughts to the discovery of those Multitude of Islands which, we are told, lay with the Tropical regions of the South of the Line and this we have on very good Authority ...'

If another ship was sent to explore the Pacific, he thought Tupaia should be included on board. The advantage over every other ship would be 'Prodigious' — Tupaia would be able to direct the navigator 'from Island to Island', ensuring a friendly reception and refreshment and allowing time 'to make his discoveries the more perfect and Compleat'.

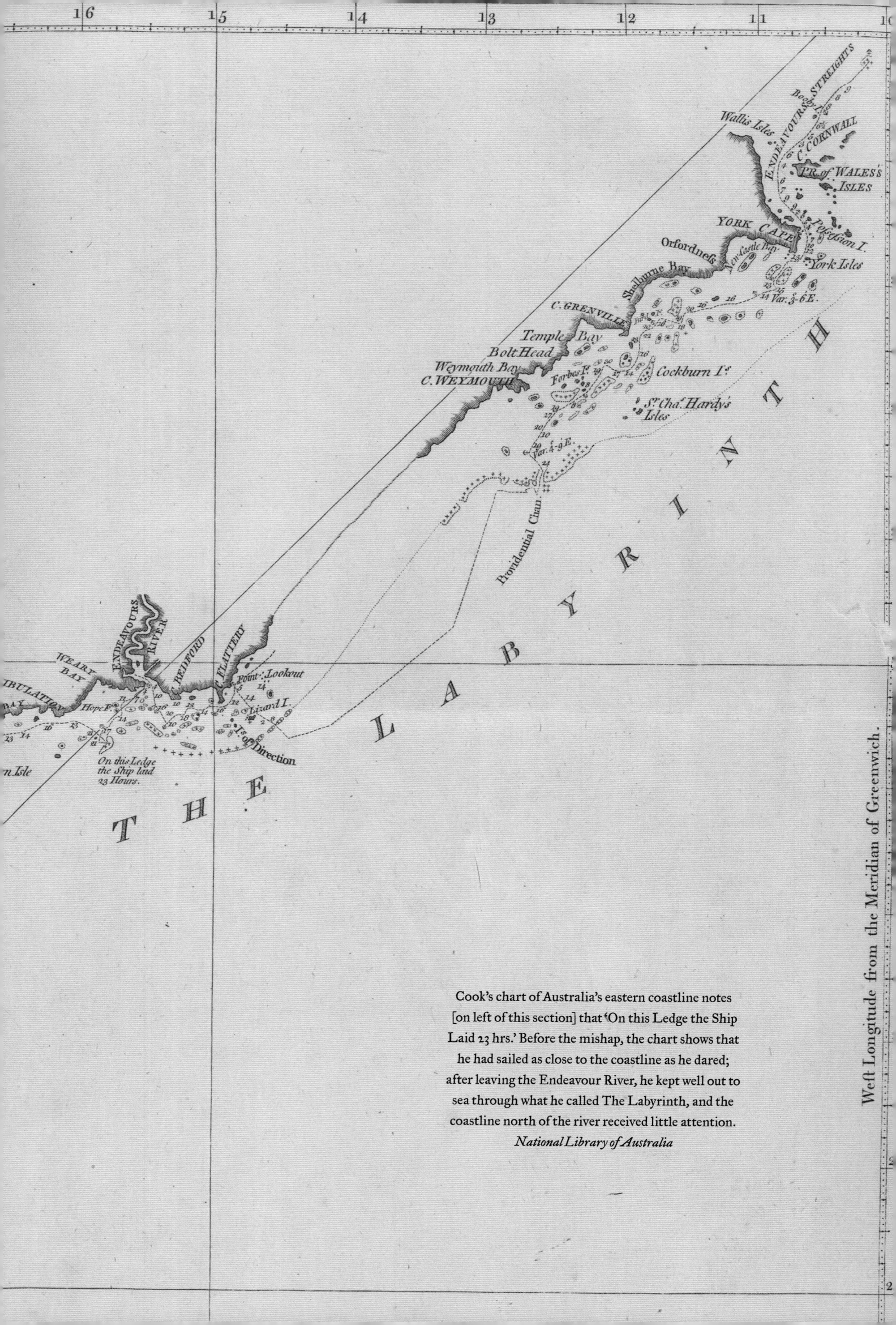

Cook's chart of Australia's eastern coastline notes [on left of this section] that 'On this Ledge the Ship Laid 23 hrs.' Before the mishap, the chart shows that he had sailed as close to the coastline as he dared; after leaving the Endeavour River, he kept well out to sea through what he called The Labyrinth, and the coastline north of the river received little attention.
National Library of Australia

9

Beyond New Zealand

Endeavour's passage westwards towards Van Diemen's Land took eighteen days. As she neared land, the Tasman Sea did its worst, with the ship battling ferocious head winds and heavy swells.

On 19 April, mate Zachary Hickes sighted a coastline, further north than Cook intended, not Van Diemen's Land at all but the uncharted coast of mainland Australia. His chart begins here, at Point Hickes [eastern Victoria]. The first landing place he named Botany Bay and the land itself, New South Wales. He then spent five months charting nearly the full length of Australia's eastern coastline, some 2000 miles.

Nowhere on Cook's first voyage did he come closer to disaster, the total loss of his ship and every man of her crew, than in the area north of today's Port Douglas. On the clear moonlit night of 11 June, on a high tide, his luck ran out.

Despite the lookouts in the crow's nest and the constant calling of the depths, the ship impaled herself on an isolated needle of the Great Barrier Reef.

Sails and yards were quickly lowered, boats put out. To lighten the ship, Cook ordered guns, water casks, iron and stone ballast and other heavy items to be thrown into the sea; totalling, he calculated, over fifty tons in weight. Men stood long exhausting shifts at the pumps.

After twenty-three hours, the stricken vessel was pulled off the reef on the high tide, but the crisis was far from over. *Endeavour* was now in mortal danger, as Cook put it, of 'going straight down'. With the ship slowly making sail towards the coast about twenty miles distant, the deadly inrushing of water must be stopped. Midshipman Jonathan Monkhouse had experience of 'fothering' — a crude but effective technique by which his seriously leaking merchant ship had made it across the Atlantic. It involved sewing tufts of wool, oakum [tarred fibre for sealing gaps] and sheep's dung into a sail and hauling it with ropes under the hull to find and plug up the holes. The young midshipman earned a special and rare mention in Cook's journal: the fothering was executed 'very much to my satisfaction'.

Now only one pump could contain the leaks. After a night at anchor and two frustrating days searching for a suitable haven, *Endeavour* was nursed into a river mouth [today's Cooktown on the Endeavour River] to be careened and repaired.

Endeavour's twelve four-pound cannons were among the heavy items thrown overboard when the ship grounded on Australia's Great Barrier Reef. One cannon was retrieved by divers in the 1970s and is now on display at the James Cook Historical Museum in Cooktown, Queensland.

It was eight weeks before Cook felt confident enough to put his ship to sea. With extreme caution, he found a way through Queensland's northern coral reefs and reached Batavia [today's Jakarta] on 11 October 1770.

There *Endeavour* was further repaired by Dutch shipwrights for the long journey home. But in this notoriously unhealthy and mosquito-ridden port, Cook's crew quickly began to fall sick with malaria and dysentery. Nearly every man was afflicted to some degree. Banks and Solander both came close to death. If Cook himself was affected, he made light of it.

Among those who died, either ashore in Batavia or soon after on the passage to Cape Town [possibly after eating bad turtle meat obtained at Princes Island in the Sunda Strait soon after leaving Batavia] were the surgeon William Monkhouse [midshipman Jonathan's older brother], the astronomer Charles Green, and the artists Sydney Parkinson and Herman

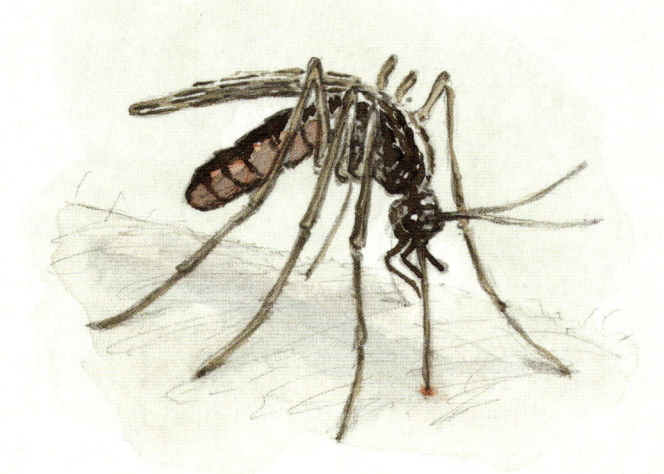

Malaria-carrying mosquitoes bred in Batavia's network of Dutch-style canals, and constant rain added to the steamy atmosphere. It was an unfortunate choice of port for the *Endeavour*.

Spöring. From the ship's company: the master Robert Molyneux, mate Zachary Hickes, two of the three young midshipmen, the corporal of marines John Truslove, the one-handed cook John Thompson, the often-drunk sailmaker John Ravenhill, carpenter John Satterly, a number of the seamen — and Banks' beloved greyhound.

Of the ninety-four men who had left from Plymouth only fifty-four would return to England.

The Tahitian boy Taiata was one of the earliest casualties, his tuberculosis aggravated by Batavia's terrible conditions. Tupaia followed soon after, heartbroken and weeping that he wished he'd never left his own country. Cook put Tupaia's death down mainly to scurvy, caused by his dislike of the ship's diet and refusal to take European medicines.

Sadly, after leaving New Zealand, Tupaia's position on the ship had become less happy. On the Australian coast, he could no more understand the Aboriginal peoples' languages than could the British. Cook wrote of him as 'shrewd, sensible and ingenious' but also as proud and obstinate. Undoubtedly his tendency to present himself to New Zealand's inhabitants as *Endeavour*'s real commander had been irritating, and he was not popular with the crew.

But it was a tragic ending — Tupaia's contribution as Pacific navigator and even more as interpreter and mediator on the New Zealand coast had been immense. He'd also shown a talent for sketching, creating what are now treasured as iconic images of Māori and European first contact.

On 26 December 1770, after three months in Batavia, *Endeavour* sailed for the Cape of Good Hope. Cook spent a month in Cape Town, hoping the time ashore would benefit his sickly crew, then four days at the island of St Helena.

Leaking badly, with hull, masts, rigging and sails in sorry condition, *Endeavour* finally anchored in the Downs on 13 July 1771. The first person to sight the English coast at Land's End was the sharp-eyed Nicholas Young.

THE SECOND VOYAGE 1772–75

Despite Cook's strenuous efforts on this first voyage to disprove the theory of the southern continent, he was not entirely convinced. Even as *Endeavour* made her way homewards up the Atlantic, he was preparing the case for a second voyage. With influential scientists and cartographers similarly doubtful, it took little persuading for the British government to order a second voyage. To lead the expedition, the obvious choice was James Cook, now promoted to Commander. Two ships were to sail in company: H.M.S. *Resolution* under Cook's command, and a second collier, the H.M.S. *Adventure*, under Tobias Furneaux.

Joseph Banks, now basking in the admiration of London society, indicated his desire to sail on *Resolution*, but he demanded extravagant modifications to the vessel to accommodate his needs and a party of no fewer than fifteen scientists with their assorted servants, musicians, and even a young woman as Banks's 'cabin boy'.

The modifications proved so unseaworthy, putting the ship in danger of capsize during her first sea trials, that Lord Sandwich, the First Lord of the Admiralty, promptly had them removed, to Cook's relief and Banks's very public fury and abrupt withdrawal from the expedition. [He went exploring in Scotland, Iceland and south Wales instead.] The ships were speedily prepared for sea and sailed from Plymouth on 13 July 1772, only a year after *Endeavour*'s return.

Cook's second voyage used Ship Cove in Queen Charlotte Sound as a base from which to explore the southern hemisphere's oceans. He took *Resolution* and *Adventure* deep into the southern Atlantic and Indian Oceans, then south to the Antarctic regions of the southern Pacific — 'not only farther than any other man has been before me, but as far as I think possible for man to go'.

These lengthy and hazardous passages through the wild 'Roaring Forties' and among Antarctica's icebergs finally and convincingly dispelled the southern continent theory.

On this voyage Cook surveyed many of the major Pacific Island groups, from New Caledonia in the west to Easter Island in the east, before arriving back at Portsmouth in July 1775. [His escort ship *Adventure*, separated from *Resolution* in a storm, had arrived back in England a year earlier.]

Cook also successfully tested the Kendall chronometer [K1], a copy by London watchmaker, Larcum Kendall, of John Harrison's great pioneering timepiece known as Harrison 4 [H4], which now enabled navigators to calculate their longitude with great accuracy.

THE THIRD AND FINAL VOYAGE 1776–1780

Despite being promoted to post-captain and showered with honours, Cook found a quiet life ashore as a naval pensioner little to his liking.

He was persuaded to command a third voyage, this time to search for the mythical northwest passage through the frozen reaches of northern America. The passage, it was believed, would provide a shorter trade route between Europe and the East. His two ships H.M.S. *Resolution* and H.M.S. *Discovery* sailed from Plymouth on 12 July 1776, arriving in Ship Cove by way of the Cape of Good Hope seven months later, on 12 February 1777.

From New Zealand, the ships sailed northeast to Tahiti and the Hawaiian islands, then undertook an extensive survey of the very northernmost regions of the Pacific, along the uncharted coasts of America, Alaska and Siberia. Voyaging in these extreme high latitudes exacted a heavy toll on the condition of the vessels, the morale of the crew, and Cook's health.

With an unhappy ship and the northwest passage proving elusive, Cook returned to Hawaii for the northern winter. On 14 February 1779, after experiencing worsening relationships with the islanders, he was bludgeoned to death on the rocky shore of Kealakekua Bay. His body was prepared by the islanders with the customary rituals accorded to chiefs, and some dismembered remains were returned to *Resolution*'s crew for formal burial at sea.

Charles Clerke, who had sailed on all three of Cook's voyages, took command of *Resolution*, followed by John Gore after Clerke's death from tuberculosis on the Siberian coast. *Resolution* and *Discovery* made a second unsuccessful attempt to locate the northwest passage, finally returning to England in October 1780.

James Cook, four marines and sixteen Hawaiians died in the angry confrontation at Kealakekua Bay. Cook, now tired, irrational and autocratic, had outstayed his welcome, while the Hawaiians had lost all respect for his chiefly and perhaps even godlike status. There is no evidence for the belief that his body was eaten; in Hawaiian culture, a dead chief's bones were revered as powerful relics.

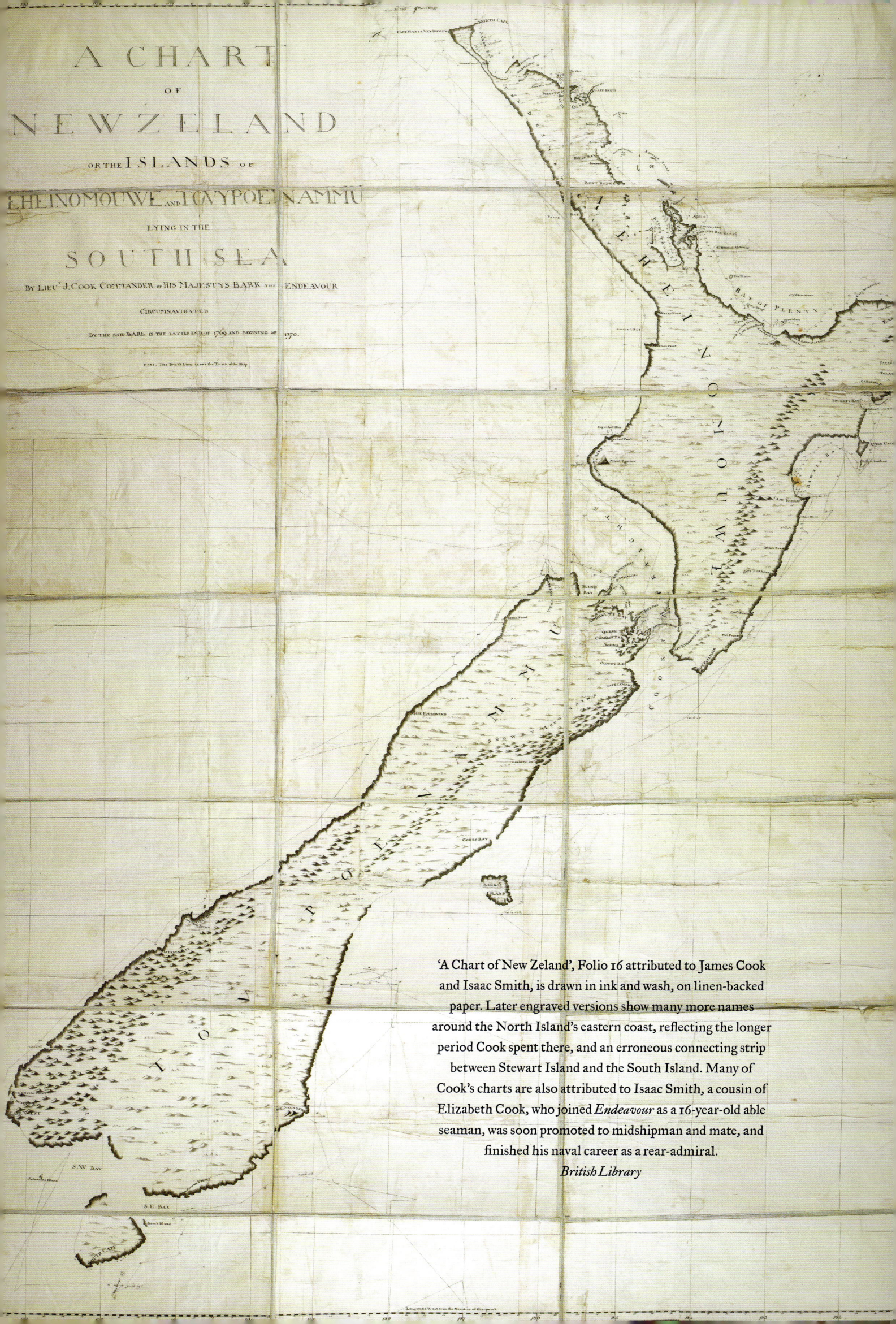

A CHART
OF
NEWZELAND
OR THE ISLANDS OF
EHEINOMOUWE AND TOVYPOENAMMU
LYING IN THE
SOUTH SEA
BY LIEU.T J. COOK COMMANDER OF HIS MAJESTYS BARK THE ENDEAVOUR

CIRCUMNAVIGATED

BY THE SAID BARK IN THE LATTER END OF 1769 AND BEGINNING OF 1770.

Note. The Dotted Lines shews the Track of the Ship

'A Chart of New Zeland', Folio 16 attributed to James Cook and Isaac Smith, is drawn in ink and wash, on linen-backed paper. Later engraved versions show many more names around the North Island's eastern coast, reflecting the longer period Cook spent there, and an erroneous connecting strip between Stewart Island and the South Island. Many of Cook's charts are also attributed to Isaac Smith, a cousin of Elizabeth Cook, who joined *Endeavour* as a 16-year-old able seaman, was soon promoted to midshipman and mate, and finished his naval career as a rear-admiral.
British Library

10

The Legacy

Sometime after leaving New Zealand in April 1771, probably on the two-week crossing of the Tasman Sea, James Cook made some helpful and modest notes about his experience of charting the two islands of New Zealand.

The journal chapter headed 'Some Account of New Zealand' gives us Cook's own thoughts about his completed chart. He points out the places where he's confident of correctness, first the lower North Island coast between Cape Palliser and East Cape, 'laid down pretty accurate'.

From East Cape to Cape Maria van Diemen, he's slightly less sure, as is shown by the dotted lines on the chart, but nonetheless he believes there's been no significant error.

From Cape Maria van Diemen south to about the latitude of Kawhia Harbour, the line of the sea coast 'may be erroneous' due to the necessity of sailing 5—8 leagues [about 20 miles] from the shore. But all the way down to Cook Strait, able to run 'near the shore all the way,' circumstances allowed him to be sure of his calculations.

'In Short, I believe that this Island [North Island] will never be found to differ Materially from the figure I have given it, and that the Coast Affords few or no Harbours but what are either taken notice of in this journal, or in some Measure pointed out in the Chart.'

He was less confident about his survey of Tovypoenammu. 'The Season of the Year and Circumstance of the Voyage would not permit me to spend so much time about this Island as I had done at the other, and the blowing weather we frequently met with made it both dangerous and difficult to keep upon the Coast.'

However, he is satisfied that from Queen Charlotte's Sound down the eastern coast to north of Banks 'Island' is 'pretty accurate'. From here to Cape Saunders and on south around the southern peninsula to Cape West he was too far offshore, and the weather too bad, to be 'Particular'. His first charts reflect his uncertainty about the southern extremities of Tovypoenammu, to the extent that portions of the coastline were left blank.

Yet, for most of the South Island's west coast, even up to Queen Charlotte's Sound, [his survey] 'will in most places be found to differ not much from the truth'.

As many books have pointed out, James Cook was not a man to blow his own trumpet. To have charted the South Island by a running survey, entirely without making land for nearly eight weeks [7 February to 27 February] was an astonishing feat of seamanship and cartography. And later surveys using superior technology have shown that Cook was seriously underestimating his achievement.

According to his biographer J.C. Beaglehole [1974], 'The important thing was the character of the man, his obstinate persistence in hanging on — to the North Cape, to Cape Maria van Diemen — till he was sure that in spite of all tempests he had got them down on his chart exactly where they ought to be.

'At the end of his circumnavigation that chart, as he found out later, was slightly out in longitude; and we know that it had a few other defects. But there had never been another chart like it in all the history of discovery. There were not many charts as good in all the atlases. And it was the fruit of six months' work …'

As Hydrographer for the Royal New Zealand Navy, Larry Robbins commanded HMNZS *Monowai* from 1994 to 1998, in charge of surveys around New Zealand and the south Pacific. His resurvey of Pickersgill Harbour in Dusky Sound in 1995 removed from a modern chart the last area directly attributed to Cook.

'Such is the high esteem that Cook and his work were held in, that the new 1997 chart, with our survey, also included Cook's original plan of the harbour from his second voyage in H.M.S. *Resolution* in 1773. Following in Cook's footsteps around many parts of the New Zealand coast, one could never fail to be impressed by what Cook and his men achieved using the instruments and ships of the day, often in appalling conditions.'

A former admiral of the Royal New Zealand Navy, J. O'C. Ross, agrees. 'The "Cook Chart" of New Zealand,' he wrote, 'was Cook's legacy to hydrography and by far his greatest achievement'. A young New Zealand navy officer had once told him, 'Give me Cook's Chart, sir, and at any time I would take a ship around the coast of New Zealand with it'.

Tributes have likewise come from Europe. Julie-Mari Crozet, navigator on Marion du Fresne's visit in 1772, later compared Cook's chart with his own. 'I found it of an exactitude and of a thoroughness of detail which astonished me beyond all powers of expression, and I doubt much whether the charts of our own French coasts are laid down with greater precision'.

And Gillian Hutchinson, former Curator of the History of Cartography at the National Maritime Museum, Greenwich, has written: 'The lengths to which Cook was prepared to go to make accurate observations, the breadth of his scope and the height of his ambition combined to transform Europeans' conceptions of the world.'

Yet Cook always remained resolutely down-to-earth about his achievements. A month after returning from the first voyage he wrote to his former employer, John Walker of Whitby.

The expectations of his superiors, he wrote, had been fully answered, and he'd had an 'extremely pleasing' hour-long conference with the King. But he added,

'I however have made no very great Discoveries yet I have explor'd more of the Great South Sea than all that have gone before me so much that little remains now to be done to have a thorough knowledge of that part of the Globe ...'

Typically, he gives credit to the support provided for his voyage by the Admiralty and the Royal Society and to 'a better ship for such a Service I never would wish for'.

James Cook and his wife Elizabeth left no children. They married in 1762, and their first child James was born in 1763, following by Nathaniel in 1764. A daughter, Elizabeth, and two further sons all died in infancy. The last child, Hugh, was born in 1776, the year Cook left for his final voyage.

Both the elder sons followed naval careers, but died tragically young. In 1780, sixteen-year-old Nathaniel was lost at sea when his ship went down off the coast of Jamaica in a hurricane. James reached the age of twenty-nine and the rank of lieutenant but in 1794 drowned in Poole Harbour, on his way back to his ship. James' death came only a few weeks after his brother Hugh, a theology student at Cambridge University, was struck down by scarlet fever, aged seventeen.

The widowed Elizabeth Cook thus survived the death of all six of her children, dying in 1835 at the age of ninety-three. A naval pension enabled her to live comfortably into old age. Before her death, she systematically gave away memorabilia connected with her husband's voyages and destroyed all his letters, papers deemed to be private and to her, sacred.

However, Cook's journals written at sea during his three great voyages survive, as originals and as edited books published in London. Other extant documents, including his charts, ships' logs and letters to and from the Admiralty, are held in museums and libraries, mostly in the UK. [As are the *Endeavour* journals of Joseph Banks and several of Cook's officers.]

The famous Cook chart wasn't the only achievement specific to New Zealand. The journals kept by Cook and Joseph Banks include detailed observations of the landscape and many aspects of Māori life and culture. These writings laid the foundations for the study of anthropology in New Zealand.

The academic study of New Zealand's natural history began with Joseph Banks and Dr Daniel Solander: not only the specimens they gathered and catalogued, but descriptions of the countryside, the trees and plants, the fish and birdlife, noting the absence of mammals besides dogs and rats. [In Australia, while *Endeavour* was being repaired, Banks recorded the first European sighting of the kangaroo.] On the domestic front, the pigs, goats and potatoes Cook left behind all thrived.

With *Endeavour*'s first voyage, Cook proved to medical scientists that scurvy could be contained by rigorous below-decks hygiene and a ship's diet that included fresh fish and greens, malt and sauerkraut, although he wasn't able to identify which items had specifically been effective.

Apart from the ill-starred Tupaia, Cook lost none of his crew to scurvy, unlike most other ships' captains of his time. By end of the eighteenth century, largely due to the pioneering clinical trials and writings of the Scottish doctor James Lind, it had been established that scurvy could be prevented by citrus fruit, especially lemons. With the discovery of vitamins in early twentieth century, the basic cause of scurvy — deficiency of Vitamin C [ascorbic acid, found principally in citrus] — was finally understood.

Endeavour's artists, notably Sydney Parkinson, left images that opened up the Pacific to European knowledge: for Banks, over 1200 botanical and zoological drawings, along with many

Elizabeth Cook, during her seventeen-year marriage, never enjoyed her husband's company for more than a year at a time. In the years before her death, she destroyed all Cook's intimate letters to her, so that little is known about his private and inner life. On her death at 94, with no surviving children to inherit, her Cook memorabilia and possessions went to relatives, friends, servants, charities and the British Museum.

landscapes and portraits [about 140 survive] done in his spare time. Tupaia's drawings and watercolours have become iconic symbols of Māori-European encounter. After the death of Alexander Buchan early in the voyage, Herman Spöring also contributed memorable sketches.

Cook's three voyages each made huge contributions to many branches of science and the arts. He is credited with mentoring young officers who further developed his techniques of surveying and navigation on explorations to many parts of the globe. These included William Bligh, George Vancouver, George Dixon, James Colnett, Nathaniel Pollock and Henry Roberts.

Museums, libraries, art galleries and private collectors, in Britain, Germany, Austria, Switzerland, Australia, Italy and America, hold extensive collections of the Pacific artefacts, specimens and memorabilia traded by those who sailed with Cook — although in some cases, artefacts have been returned to their country or people of origin.

Museums around the world pay their special tributes. In Yorkshire, there's the Captain Cook Memorial Museum in Whitby, while the Captain Cook Schoolroom Museum in Great Ayton preserves the village school he attended. In Melbourne can be found the family cottage of Cook's father John, shipped there from Great Ayton in 1934. In north Queensland, the James Cook Museum at Cooktown is close to the riverbank where the crippled *Endeavour* was careened for repairs in 1770.

James Cook is personally remembered in many countries — his name given to landmarks, islands, townships, wharves, universities, schools, hospitals, libraries, chapels, taverns, businesses, streets, ships, coins, even a crater on the moon.

Full-size statues and obelisks to his memory have been erected in New Zealand, Australia, Britain, Canada, Hawaii and elsewhere, many marking his landing places around the Pacific. A simple white monument stands on Point Venus in Tahiti, and the exact site of his death on the beach of Kealakekua Bay in Hawai'i is marked by a plaque set into the foreshore rocks.

Hundreds of biographies and studies have examined his life and voyages. The best-known paintings, by Nathanial Dance and John Webber, both from 1776, show him in formal uniform and reveal little of his character. Only the brooding portrait by William Hodges, painted maybe a little earlier, thought lost but rediscovered in 1986, hints at a less forbidding, more introspective personality.

Perhaps the greatest tribute to his Pacific explorations is the magnificent *Endeavour* replica, launched in Fremantle, Western Australia, in 1993 and widely regarded as the world's most authentic replica of an eighteenth century fully rigged ship.

In 1994, to celebrate the 225th anniversary of Cook's first voyage, *Endeavour* sailed to Cooktown and crossed the Tasman to circumnavigate New Zealand.

She then undertook an epic four-year world voyage, sailing to the UK via Cape Town, and across the Atlantic to northern America. Further world voyages have taken her around Cape

Horn to visit European ports and the islands of the northern Atlantic. The *Endeavour* replica is now berthed at the Australian Maritime Museum in Sydney.

As for the original H.M.Bark *Endeavour*, after Cook she was largely forgotten. She made voyages to the Falkland Islands, Russia, and to the American civil war as a transport ship. In 1778 she was one of thirteen vessels sunk as a blockade at the entrance to Newport Harbour.

Recent archaeological research by the Rhodes Island Marine Archeology Project suggests that she lies with five others on the seafloor off Rhode Island, Newport, prompting hopes in USA and UK that some remains and artifacts may be recovered for museum display. A second organisation, the Foundation for the Preservation of Captain Cook's Ships, has been formed to investigate the fate of Cook's *Resolution*, sold to the French and renamed *La Liberté*, and believed sunk in Newport harbour sometime after 1793.

POSTSCRIPT

Since James Cook's circumnavigation of the uncharted islands of New Zealand and the publication of his chart in 1772, there have been more than 2300 shipwrecks recorded on the New Zealand coast.

This figure doesn't include many small trading vessels, nor the loss of waka in pre-European times, which are recorded in Māori oral traditions.

Cook's achievement is even more impressive in the light of this sad record: these vessels came to grief despite their masters having more navigational aids than Cook, more efficient rigs, weather forecasts and [since the 1870s] steam and diesel engines, along with permanently installed coastal lighthouses, buoys, beacons, lighted shipping lanes, and of course, always to hand, their all-important charts, today on large screens.

Through the early days of New Zealand exploration and settlement by Europeans, Cook's 1772 charts sufficed. Not until the mid-1800s, eighty years after Cook, were New Zealand's coasts again surveyed, this time by Captain John L. Stokes in H.M.S. *Acheron* and Commander Byron Drury in H.M.S. *Pandora*. In the twentieth century, official charts have been produced by naval hydrographic survey ships. Even today, sophisticated electronic instruments like depth sounders, radar, GPS navigation systems and 24-hour satellite weather forecasting are no guarantee against poor seamanship or faulty navigation, or the calms, huge waves and fierce gales that can drive ships onto unforgiving coastlines.

A CHART
OF
NEW ZELAND
OR THE ISLANDS OF
AEHEINOMOUWE AND TOVYPOENAMMU
LYING IN THE
SOUTH SEA
BY LIEUT. J. COOK COMMANDER OF HIS MAJESTY'S BARK THE ENDEAVOUR
CIRCUMNAVIGATED
IN THE SAID BARK, IN THE LATTER END OF 1769 AND BEGINNING OF 1770

James Cook's chart published in 1773 is here superimposed on the red outline of New Zealand as shown on today's charts. This clearly demonstrates how accurately he calculated the longitude and latitude of the country's three major islands set in the vast southern Pacific Ocean.

Bibliography

Website of the Captain Cook Society, www.captaincooksociety.com

Anderson, Atholl, Binney, Judith, Harris, Aroha, *Tangata Whenua: An Illustrated History*, Bridget Williams Books, Wellington, 2014

Banks, Joseph, *The Endeavour Journal of Sir Joseph Banks*, downloadable at gutenberg.net.au/ebooks05/0501141h.html

Beaglehole, J.C., *The Life of Captain James Cook*, Adam & Charles Black, London, 1974

Begg, A. Charles and Begg, Neil C., *James Cook and New Zealand*, A.N. Shearer, Government Printer, Wellington, 1969

Cook, James, *The Journals of Captain James Cook on his voyages of discovery*, edited from the original manuscripts by J.C. Beaglehole, Hakluyt Society, London, 1955

Cook, James, *Captain Cook in New Zealand, extracts from the journals of Captain James Cook, giving a full account in his own words of his adventures and discoveries in New Zealand*, edited by A.H. & A.W. Reed, 2nd ed, A.H. & A.W. Reed, Wellington, 1969

Cook, James, *Journal of first voyage 1768–71*, downloadable at gutenberg.net.au/ebooks/e00043.html

David, Andrew [chief editor], *The Charts & Coastal Views of Captain Cook's Voyages. Volume one: the Voyage of the Endeavour, 1768–1771*, Hakluyt Society, London, 1988

Druett, Joan, *Tupaia: The Remarkable Story of Captain Cook's Polynesian Navigator*, Penguin, Auckland, 2011

Gascoigne, John, *Captain Cook: voyager between worlds*, Hambledon Continuum, London, 2007

Kaeppler, Adrienne L., *James Cook and the Exploration of the Pacific*, Thames & Hudson, London, 2009

Lay, Graeme, the James Cook trilogy [fiction]: *The Secret Life of James Cook, James Cook's New World, James Cook's Lost World*, HarperCollins New Zealand, Auckland, 2013, 2014, 2015

Lay, Graeme, *A Travel Guide to Captain James Cook's New Zealand*, New Holland, 2017

Maling, P.B., *Historic Charts & Maps of New Zealand 1642 to 1875*, Reed Books, Auckland, 1996

Moore, Peter, *Endeavour: The Ship and the Attitude That Changed the World*, Chatto/Penguin New Zealand, 2018

O'Sullivan, Dan, *In Search of Captain Cook: Exploring the Man Through His Own Words*, I.B. Tauris & Co Ltd, London, 2008

Parkin, Ray, *H.M. Bark Endeavour: Her Place in Australian History*, Melbourne University Publishing, Melbourne, 1997

Reed, A.W., *The Reed Dictionary of New Zealand Place names* [first published 1975, new edition Peter Dowling [editor], Reed Books, Auckland, 2002

Robson, John, *Captain Cook's world: maps of the life and voyages of James Cook R.N.*, Random House, Auckland 2000

Robson, John, *The Captain Cook Encyclopaedia*, Random House New Zealand, Auckland, 2004

Robson, John, *Captain Cook's War and Peace: the Royal Navy years, 1755–1768*. Barnsley, U.K., Seaforth Publishing, 2009

Ross, J. O'C., *This Stern Coast*, A.H. & A.W. Reed, Auckland, 1969

Salmond, Anne, *Two Worlds: First Meetings Between Māori and Europeans 1642–1772*, Viking, Auckland, 1991

Salmond, Anne, *The Trial of the Cannibal Dog: Captain Cook in the South Seas*, Allen Lane, London, 2003

Salmond, Anne, *Tears of Rangi: Experiments Across Worlds*, Auckland University Press, Auckland, 2017

Thomas, Nicholas, *Discoveries: the Voyages of Captain Cook*, Allen Lane, London, 2003

Thomas, Nicholas, *The Voyages of Captain James Cook: the illustrated accounts of three epic voyages*, Voyageur Press, Quarto Publishing Group, 2016

Villiers, Alan, *James Cook: The Seamen's Seaman – a Study of the Great Discoverer*, Penguin Books, London, 1967, 2001

Acknowledgements

TESSA DUDER

Long fascinated by James Cook's iconic 'New Zeland' chart and with some experience of sailing on a modern square-rigger, I set out to write a straightforward account of Lieutenant James Cook's circumnavigation over the summer of 1769-70. The focus was to be on how the famous chart was created during those six months, and at what cost to him, his crew and ship.

During the two years this book has been in preparation, there has been increasing debate around James Cook's place in New Zealand history. We have – not before time – stopped talking about his voyages of 'discovery' and Tupaia's role during the circumnavigation is now being properly acknowledged. To mark the 250th anniversary of *Endeavour*'s landfall on the New Zealand coast in October 1769, the Government is funding local organisers to mount events for *Tuia – Encounters 250*, featuring Australia's magnificent *Endeavour* replica. To many, Cook remains one of the world's greatest explorers, surveyors and seamen, and his charting of New Zealand reason enough to celebrate. Others, however, see Cook as a murderer and an invader, the forerunner and cause of the many ills of 19th century Pacific colonialisation.

For help in keeping me on a middle course through the shoals of opposing viewpoints, I am grateful to John Robson, former map librarian at the University of Waikato and president of the international Captain Cook Society. Conversations with him reinforced the scholarship to be found in his three invaluable books on Cook [see the bibliography for titles], along with his much appreciated comments on the manuscript. Among the hundreds published, J.C. Beaglehole and Anne Salmond's classic works on Cook are of special value. [Any errors that remain are of course mine alone.]

Thanks also go to the British Library and National Library of Australia for use of charts; to former Royal New Zealand Navy surveyor Larry Robbins and square-rig enthusiast John Duder; and particularly, to illustrator David Elliot for his contribution of both splendid artworks and suggestions for the book's design.

DAVID ELLIOT

I would like to acknowledge the artists Sydney Parkinson, Herman Spöring, Tupaia, Nathaniel Dance and Ray Parkin, whose work has been the basis of many of the illustrations. Thanks also to John Dikkenberg, Master of H.M.B. *Endeavour*, Australian Maritime Museum; Maggie Patton, State Library of New South Wales; Dr Donald Kerr, Special Collections Librarian, University of Otago; Karen Craw, Maps Curator, Hocken Collections and Dr Gillian Elliot for their generous advice and support.

Index

Acheron, H.M.S., 90
Adventure, H.M.S., 98
Alaska, 99
Antarctic regions, 98
Atlantic Ocean, 7, 12, 98, 105
Austral Islands, 27

Banks, Joseph, 6, 10, 13, 16, 18, 19, 20, 21, 24, 27, 33, 34, 40, 42, 43, 48, 54, 59, 65, 72, 73, 74, 84, 85, 89, 92, 96, 98, 103, 104
Banks Peninsula, 5
Bay of Biscay, 64
Beaglehole, J.C., 5, 43, 103
Bligh, Capt. William, 105
Bora Bora, 25
Botany Bay, 95
Brett, Sir Piercy, 58
British Library, 5, 23, 44
Buchan, Alexander, 13, 35, 104

Canada, 11, 12
Canary Islands, 69
Cape Horn, 8, 20, 92, 106
Cape Kidnapper, 40
Cape of Good Hope, 92, 93, 97, 99
Cape Maria van Diemen, 8, 65, 101
Cape Town, 96, 105
Captain Cook Schoolroom Museum, Great Ayton, 105
Clerke, Captain Charles, 12, 99
Cook, Elizabeth [wife], 8, 9, 103, 104
Cook, Elizabeth [daughter], 10
Cook, Hugh, 103
Cook, James [son], 103,
Cook, Joseph [son], 10, 103
Cook, Lieutenant James,
  • early life, 12, 13
  • early career, 11, 12
  • in Canada, Newfoundland, 11
  • in Tiera del Fuego, 20
  • in Tahiti, Matavai Bay, 18, 20, 21-24
  • and Transit of Venus, 8, 11, 16, 19, 21
  • and his New Zealand names, 10, 44
  • and 'Cook's Straights', 10, 75
  • at Tūranganui-a-Kiwa [Poverty Bay], 27, 29-35
  • in Hawkes Bay, 39-42
  • at Anaura, Uawa/Tolaga Bay, 43-44
  • at Whitianga, Mercury Bay, 44-49
  • at Thames, Waihou River, 51, 52-53
  • in Hauraki Gulf, 51, 56, 57
  • at Bream Bay [Whangarei], 57
  • at Bay of Islands [Tokerau], 51, 58-63
  • rounding North Cape, Cape Maria van Diemen, 64-68
  • charting North Island west coast, 68-69
  • at Ship Cove/Meretoto, 71-76
  • at Totara-nui/Queen Charlotte's Sound, 71, 73
  • charting South Island east coast, 78-85
  • rounding South Cape, 85-88
  • charting West Coast, 88-91
  • at Admiralty [Murderer's] Bay, 90-93
  • charting New Holland [Australia], 13, 95-96
  • in Batavia [Jakarta], 7, 96-97
  • return to UK, 92-97
  • second voyage, 98
  • third voyage, 99
  • death in Kealakekua Bay, 99
  • as surveyor, cartographer, 37, 101-103
  • as purser, 16
  • and aids to navigation, 25, 30, 37, 38, 55, 56, 91
  • and cannibalism, 34, 39, 43, 73
  • and ship discipline, 60, 55
  • and scurvy, 11, 16, 21, 28, 49, 68, 97, 104
  • his journal of the first voyage, 5, 6, 8, 20, 23, 24, 25, 28, 35, 40, 57, 59, 63, 65, 68, 73, 75, 79, 85, 86, 90, 92, 93, 95, 101, 103
  • his 'Chart of New Zeland', Folio 16, 5, 6, 90, 91, 92, 100
  • and family, 10, 103
  • portraits, 9, 105
Cooktown [Queensland], 95
Cox, Matthew, 60
Crozet, Julie-Mari, 102

Dalrymple, Alexander, 8, 11, 13
Dance, Nathaniel, 5, 9, 105
De Surville, Jean François Marie, 68
Deptford [naval dockyard], 16
Discovery, H.M.S., 99
Dolphin, H.M.S., 13, 19, 20
Drury, Commander Byron, 106

Earl of Pembroke [ship], 13
Egmont, Mt [Taranaki], 10, 28, 69
Endeavour, H.M.B.,
  • specifications 13, 14-15
  • provisions/gear on board, 16
  • careening, 69, 71
  • near disasters in New Zealand, 59, 63, 65, 76-8, 82-3, 86, 90
  • grounding on Great Barrier Reef, 95
  • repairs in Batavia, 96
  • further history, 106
Endeavour replica, Sydney, 106

Falkland Islands, 106
Foundation for the Preservation of Captain Cook's Ships, 106
France, 6, 64
Furneaux, Captain Tobias, 98

George III, 5, 11, 31, 49, 73
Gore, Lieutenant John, 12, 33, 47, 84, 99
Green, Charles, 16, 20, 21, 43, 46, 96
Grenville H.M.S., 12

Harrison, John, 99
Hawaiian Islands, 99
Hawke, Sir Edward, 39
Heemskerk [ship], 69
Hickes, Lieutenant Zachary, 55, 59, 95, 97
Hodges, William, 9, 105
Horeta Te Taniwha, 48
Hutchinson, Gillian, 102

Indian Ocean, 92

James Cook Historical Museum, Cooktown, 96, 105

Kendal, Larcum, 98

La Liberte [ship], 106
Lind, Dr James, 104
Lord Sandwich H.M.S. [formerly *Endeavour*] 106

Madeira, 20
Manley, Isaac, 13, 24
Maskelyne, Nevil, 20
Milton, John, 42
Molyneux, Robert, 12, 97
Monkhouse, Jonathon, 95, 96
Monkhouse, William, 97
Morton, James, Earl of, 19, 20, 21, 34

Natural History Museum, London, 42
National Library of Australia, 94
National Maritime Museum, Greenwich, 102
New Holland [Australia], 8, 12, 13, 19, 65, 92
Newfoundland, 11, 12
Newport, Rhode Island [USA], 106

Palliser, Sir Hugh, 11
Pandora H.M.S., 106
Paradise Lost [poem], 42

Parkinson, Sydney, 6, 13, 24, 35, 40, 45, 60, 97, 104
Pegasus H.M.S., 86
Pembroke, H.M.S., 12, 13
Peru, 68
Pickersgill, Richard, 8, 63, 102
Plymouth, 10, 11, 17
Port Douglas, 95
Portland, 39

Queen Charlotte's Sound, 73, 76, 89, 98, 101

Ra'iātea, 25
Ravenhill, John, 13, 97
Resolution, H.M.S., 89, 99, 102
Rhode Island Marine Archeology Project, 106
Rio de Janiero, 20, 21
Robbins, Commander Larry, 102
Ross, Admiral, J.O'C, 102
Royal Navy, 7, 11, 12, 13, 54
Royal Society, 5, 11, 13, 19, 21, 100, 103

Salmond, Anne, 35
Samoa, 25
Sandwich, Lord, 98
Siberia, 99
Smith, Isaac, 8
Solander, Dr Daniel, 13, 16, 21, 35, 42, 43, 44, 28, 54, 55, 59, 74, 92, 103
Spöring, Herman, 13, 30, 35, 40, 43, 46, 60, 97, 104, 105
St Helena, 7, 8, 97
St John Baptiste [ship], 68
Staithes, 12
Stephens, Philip, 7, 8, 10, 92
Stewart Island, 5, 82
Stewart, William, 86
Stokes, Captain J.L., 90, 106

Tahiti, 8, 11, 18, 19, 20, 21, 23, 71
Taiata, 24, 27, 39, 97
Tasman, Captain Abel, 8, 11, 12, 19, 25, 28, 69, 76, 90
Tasman Sea, 64, 91, 95, 101
tattooing, 21, 33, 43, 57, 58, 73, 74
Tauhu, 18, 21
Te Makura, 35

Te Maro, 34, 34
Te Papa Tongarewa, Museum of New Zealand, 9
Te Rakau, 34, 35
Terra Australis Incognita, 5, 7, 8, 19, 28, 87, 92
Thompson, John, 97
Tonga, 25, 65
Topaa, 71, 75, 76
Truslove, John, 97
Tupaia, 6, 23, 25, 27, 33, 34, 39, 43, 48, 54, 55, 59, 71, 73, 75, 76, 93, 97, 104
Tupaia's Chart of Pacific Islands, 22-23, 25

Vancouver, George, 105
Van Diemen's Land, 92
Visscher, François, 8, 11, 76

Waitematā Harbour, 57
Walker, Captain James, 12, 102
Wallis, Captain Samuel, 8, 19, 20, 25
Webber, John, 9, 105
Whitby, 12

Young, Nicholas, 12, 24, 29, 30, 97

Zeehaen [ship], 69